KILIMS

DECORATING WITH TRIBAL RUGS

KILIMS

ELIZABETH HILLIARD

SOMA

First published 1999 by Pavilion Books Limited. North American edition published 1999
by Soma Books, by arrangement with Pavilion Books Limited.

Soma Books is an imprint of Bay Books & Tapes, 555 De Haro St., No. 220,
San Francisco, CA 94107.

For the Pavilion Books edition:
Design: David Fordham
Picture Research: Mary-Jane Gibson

For the Soma Edition:
Publisher: James Connolly
Production: Suzanne Scott
North American Editor: Heather Garnos

Library of Congress Cataloging-in-Publication Data on file with publisher

ISBN 1-57959-019-5

Printed in Singapore
10 9 8 7 6 5 4 3 2 1

Distributed by Publishers Group West

CONTENTS

INTRODUCTION

THERE IS A DREAM WE ALL HAVE, of an old house with beamed ceilings and polished wooden floors. It is furnished with antiques and comfortable upholstered chairs. Framed paintings hang on the walls, the delicate scent of lavender hangs in the air, and a fire crackles in the fireplace. On the table there is a pot of tea and a plate of warm, buttery pastries. On the floor there is, inevitably, a Persian carpet. Its rich colors and intricate design contribute to the mellow, well-worn, much-loved appearance of the room.

This is a picture of tranquillity and completeness, qualities that most of us would like more of in our homes, and in our lives. We may not be able to acquire the whole package – beamed house, antique furniture, and all – but today there is no shortage of Persian rugs for the having. A rug, well designed and well made, is a wonderful thing to own. On any sort of floor, but especially on natural floorings like wood or stone, a rug adds comfort. It can also pull a room together, giving it a focus and drawing the various parts into a whole.

Another image springs to mind: a contemporary, modern interior, light, white, and gleaming. The picture is enlivened with splashes of brilliant color – some cushions on the sofa, a vase of flowers, a vibrant kilim on the floor. The timeless designs of kilims are as much at home in a modern interior, adding a touch of softness underfoot, as they are in older, traditional homes.

Persian tribal rugs and kilims are not only beautiful in themselves, they are also precious artifacts. Sitting on rugs in a shady nomad's tent on a mountainside in southern Iran, sipping tea and looking out on the magnificence of the sandy, chiseled landscape, it is difficult to believe that this way of life will not continue forever. After all, the lifestyle of Iran's tribal nomads has not changed fundamentally in the past two thousand years or more. But it may not survive much longer, as the pressures of the modern

BELOW When they migrate, the Kashgai tribespeople pack up their belongings in bags faced with small woven pieces such as this.

10

RIGHT A pile of rolled-up, handsome Kashgai or Shiraz rugs.

FAR RIGHT Runners like this, made in Karaja in northwest Iran, where the weavers speak Turkish, are useful in halls and passageways.

world come to bear. Once gone, it can never be regained. All that will remain will be the rugs.

Tribal rugs are all woven by women, who card, spin, dye, and weave the wool as part of their everyday domestic activities. The quality of design and execution varies hugely, but the best rugs take your breath away. The women make not only rugs with traditional patterns, those which immediately come to mind when we think of a "Persian rug." They also weave kilims with vivid colors and dynamic geometric patterns. And they create bright new gabbehs with a luxurious deep pile. They have, by heritage, not only the skills needed to make rugs (and the wool, which comes from their sheep) but a gift for design and decoration. The best rugs are works of tribal art.

Contemporary decoration calls for flexibility and choice. Today's Persian tribal rugs and kilims offer both in great wealth. They are the latest creations in a story of rug-making that goes back . . . well, we know not how far, but thousands of years at the very least. To have a rug of this type in your home is to own a piece of history.

SECTION I:

HISTORY AND CONTEXT

Opposite Fairly typical of rugs made in the town of Tabriz, this piece was probably made in the late nineteenth or early twentieth century.

Left Rugs of this size that display this degree of detail in their pattern are made in workshops rather than on a hillside by nomads. Tehran housewives favor these paler colors.

RUGS THROUGH HISTORY

OPPOSITE The Pazyryk Rug, now in the Hermitage Museum in St. Petersburg, is significant as the only existing rug example from before the middle of the sixteenth century. It takes its name from the Pazyryk Valley in southern Siberia, where it was found in the late 1940s.

RIGHT A "serapi" carpet (this is the name usually given to old rugs made in northwest Iran or Heriz).

THE HISTORY OF RUGS, from their origin until the second half of the sixteenth century, is simple to grasp, because only one rug survives. Know the name and story of that (the Pazyryk Rug, now in the Hermitage Museum, St. Petersburg) and one other outstandingly famous rug, the enormous Ardebil Carpet (in the Victoria & Albert Museum, London), and you can talk convincingly about the origins of Persian rugs.

Of course, there is much more to the history of rugs than simply these two pieces, but until the last few centuries all history is speculation, albeit based largely on sound evidence. The inlaid floors of ancient palaces, Greek and Latin manuscripts, carved stone friezes, the design and construction of the Pazyryk Rug itself . . . together these add up to a picture of an art and craft with a long and impressive tradition.

The tale of the Pazyryk Rug is extraordinary. One of the reasons why no other rugs have survived is that, compared to ironwork, for example, or pottery that has been fired in a kiln, textiles are more perishable over millennia, especially in times of war or upheaval, when their preservation is not the first thought on people's minds. This rug, however, survived because it was accidentally preserved by being frozen.

To explain how this happened, we have to go back to Central Asia in the fifth century BC. As in some other cultures, when rulers in this region died

15

and were buried, they were entombed with sufficient possessions to more than ensure their comfort and prestige in the world to come. When one particular Scythian prince or king was buried in the Pazyryk Valley in southern Siberia, the fame of the wealth with which he was buried caused his tomb to be the target of robbers shortly after his death. They stole precious stones and gold, but left the rest. In the act of theft they broke the seal on the tomb, so that it subsequently flooded. The water froze, preserving the contents for what could have been indefinite thousands of years.

In the late 1940s, however, a Russian archaeologist named S.J. Rudenko and his team explored the area and excavated this particular tomb. They could not have guessed what they would find, though if they had dreamed of fabulous riches to compare with the tomb of Tutankhamun in Egypt, discovered in the 1920s, they would have been disappointed. To scholars, however, the discovery of a rug an astonishing 2,400 years old (roughly) was equally valuable.

Amongst many other artifacts and objects, including kilim-type flatweaves and felt rugs, they found what came to be known as the Pazyryk Rug (sometimes also called the "Altai Rug," on account of the location of the tomb in the Altai Mountains). A thing of beauty in itself, this was the first concrete piece of evidence of textile art before the sixteenth century.

The Pazyryk Rug is almost square, about 6 x 6 feet, and the design is a visually appealing combination of geometric structure (many straight borders, and the central field divided into squared-off sections) and details which, if not curvilinear (see page 25), are not geometric either (lifelike elks and horses portrayed marching around the borders). The full-blown curvilinear style, with ornate curlicues and arabesques, did not emerge until the fifteenth century, as we shall see.

The success of the design of the Pazyryk Rug lies partly in the fact that it is so well balanced — each wide border has matching slim borders on each side, and the elks marching in one direction are balanced by the horses going the opposite way round the rug (seven horses on each side representing the number buried with a Scythian warrior). The stylized flowers with leaves that occupy the center squares are echoed by smaller versions of the same in one of the first borders to surround them.

The colors, too, are attractive and well-planned. The central area has a pinkish, terracotta background, while borders are decorated in blue, yellow, and the same pink as the field. There is no way of knowing who planned this design or made the Pazyryk Rug. Its dating is based on archaeological information.

All in all, the Pazyryk Rug speaks to us not only of the talented individual designer and technically accomplished weaver who made it, but also of a thriving tradition of textile art in general and woven floorcoverings in particular. It is unbelievable that this rug sprang fully-formed from the skills of individuals — rather it is the culmination of many centuries of developing craftsmanship.

Ancient texts, including the Old Testament of the Bible, mention rugs, as do Homer's *Iliad* and other Greek and Latin texts, though the Latin word "tapetum" can also be translated to mean curtain or hanging. The Assyrian palace of Nineveh, which is a century or two older than the Pazyryk Rug, was decorated with carved stone slabs whose pattern is strongly reminiscent of the quatrefoil design in the central sections of the Pazyryk Rug. Other evidence lies on the floors of Roman and earlier villas, where stone and mosaic inlaid patterns replicate the design of decorative rugs. In Iran itself, rugs feature in a carved stone relief at Persepolis.

About an hour's drive from the southern Iranian town of Shiraz, an important center for the sale of tribal rugs today, are the ruins of the astonishing palace of Persepolis. More a town than a palace, Persepolis was constructed in about 500 BC on a terrace of rock on a mountainside, a showpiece demonstrating the power and regional dominance of its creator, the emperor Darius. Its commanding position was reached by massive stone staircases, with steps of gentle height to allow, it is said, horsemen to ride directly up to the great gate.

Throughout the palace, walls were carved with splendid friezes depicting a wide range of activities and people. One image of Darius himself had neck and wrists encased with gold, riveted into the wall. Elsewhere friezes show visitors bringing the ruler gifts, including rugs folded over their arms and borne before them with due ceremony. By this time the ruler may have been Darius's son, Xerxes, who continued the great work at Persepolis.

Darius' empire was broken up in 330 BC as a consequence of Alexander the Great's conquest of Persia. The next flowering of Persian culture was many centuries later, in the sixteenth century AD, when Shah Abbas was ruler of Persia. This leads us to the second great rug in history, the Ardebil Carpet, created in his reign.

17

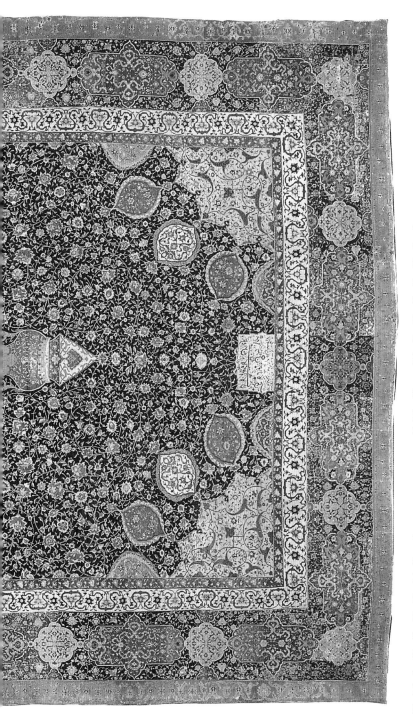

LEFT The enormous and beautifully intricate Ardebil Carpet, now in the Victoria & Albert Museum, London, is probably the most important rug in history, alongside the Pazyryk Rug. It is thought to have been made for the burial place of the founder of the illustrious Safavid dynasty and is finely worked in wool on silk warp and weft threads.

The scale of the Ardebil Carpet is impressive. At the cavernous Victoria & Albert Museum in London, it takes up almost an entire wall, filling it with the luxurious swirls of tendril and leaf and elaborate medallions and pendants that make up its design. It is 11½ yards long and 5¾ yards wide, and has a warp and weft made of silk threads. The fineness of the work is inspiring. In each inch across its width there are an average of 35 warp threads, and in each square inch of wool pile there are roughly 340 knots.

Unlike the Pazyryk Rug, the Ardebil Carpet can be ascribed to an individual craftsman, due to his signature. In a white panel at one end is the inscription drawn from a poem by the fourteenth century poet Hafiz, translated by Rexford Stead:

Except for thy haven, there is no refuge for me in this world
Other than here, there is no place for my head.
The work of a servant of the Court, Maqsud of Kashan, 946.

The date equates to 1539–40 AD. The origins of this carpet and a matching one – which is now in the Los Angeles County Museum of Art – are not certain, but they are thought to have furnished the burial place at Ardebil (hence the name) of the founder of the Safavid dynasty of which Shah Abbas was the most illustrious member. Another theory (which has not altered the name by which the rug is known) is that the carpets were made for the mosque of Imam Riza in Mashad. (This Imam's brothers, incidentally, are buried in Shiraz, an important town for tribal rugs.)

LEFT No rugs survive from this period, so miniatures such as this exquisite example give us some of our only information about the early design and use of rugs. In this illustration, probably from the fourteenth century, a ruler sits on one rug in a "kalleh," a pavilion for entertaining, while one of his entourage kneels on another, offering a dish of fruit.

Shah Abbas made Isphahan his capital, and set about transforming it into a beautiful and cultured city where all the arts thrived. Palaces and mosques were built, then decorated and furnished by the finest craftsmen. Tiles, ceramics, textiles, leatherwork, woodcarving, miniature painting . . . these and all the visual arts played their part.

For his part, Shah Abbas established a court factory. This produced quantities of rugs, not only for the king's own palaces, but also for the apartments and workplaces of his courtiers and officials. He is also believed to have presented finely woven carpets to illustrious foreigners who visited him, and to their ambassadors.

The Ardebil Carpet illustrates an interesting development in the design of rugs in the fifteenth century. With its central medallion and elaborate spandrels, it is reminiscent of tooled decoration on the cover of a leather-bound book, by which this type of rug design was inspired. The complicated and detailed patterning on the field of the rug, which is carefully calculated as if drawn on layers of tracing paper laid on top of each other, is meanwhile related to the style of the miniature painting of the Safavid court.

The expense of creating such a huge and fine carpet could only be borne by a man or court of great wealth. What became of it after the dissolution of the Safavid rule, when Afghans invaded Persia in 1721 and destroyed almost all vestiges of its culture, is not known.

In the early 1890s, however, both Ardebil Carpets appeared for sale. The one in the V&A Museum was bought by them

RIGHT A Kerman vase carpet from south-eastern Iran. The vase design is perennially popular.

RIGHT A section of the Chelsea Carpet, now in the Victoria & Albert Museum in London, is so called because it was bought from a dealer in the King's Road. This design includes two medallions (only one of which we see here) and was much copied, in India particularly.

on the advice of the celebrated designer William Morris, from Vincent Robinson & Co., who in turn had bought it from Ziegler & Co. (more about them later, on page 83) in Persia. The purchase was only possible with the aid of financial contributions from the British public. Of the two Ardebils, only one is complete (the V&A carpet), the other having been cut up in order to repair the first.

The Safavid period in Persian history was one of great fertility for carpets. Besides the Ardebils, there are several others that are worth going to see if you find yourself in one of the cities where they are now displayed in museums. One is in the Austrian capital, Vienna.

This, a "hunting carpet," is so-called not because it was taken to lay on the ground when a noble huntsman paused in the chase for refreshment, but rather because it shows a hunting scene. Hunting scenes provide one of the classic designs on Persian rugs of the sixteenth century; this one shows men with a variety of weapons including spears and bows attacking an astonishing collection of animals including leopards, bears, and antelope. The border is also famed for its beauty. Against a red background, it shows figures resembling angels, giving and receiving gifts of fruit. The Viennese hunting carpet is also interesting because, unusually, it is made entirely of silk — warps, wefts, and all.

The vase design, with flowers emerging from a single vase shape, was also popular. Like the hunting scene, it continues to appear on Persian rugs and carpets to this day. The most famous vase carpet is probably the one that was owned by William Morris himself, now hanging alongside the Ardebil Carpet in the V&A in London (as does the Chelsea Carpet). There is also a famous carpet in the Metropolitan Museum in New York: this has a bold simplicity of design and is unusual on account of its border, which is largely occupied by a long inscription going all around the edge.

RIGHT In this Turkish miniature, Suleyman the Magnificent (1494-1566) sits on a rug. The rug has a distinctive motif of three dots or circles that appears on Turkish rugs exclusively.

One other great carpet in the history of Persian rugs is different from all the rest, because it exists only in our imagination. Around the middle of the sixth century, the Persian king Chosroes I defeated the Romans and conquered areas of southern Arabia. To celebrate these momentous events and to demonstrate his power and wealth, the king is believed to have commanded the creation of an astonishing carpet around 400 x 100 feet in size, for his palace at Ctesiphon.

Probably a flatweave rather than a pile carpet, it is known as the Spring Carpet of King Chosroes and portrayed a garden with paths and streams separating areas of trees and flower beds. It is supposed to have been encrusted with precious stones and embroidery in gold and silver thread. This fabulous piece is said to have been destroyed by being cut up into pieces less than a hundred years later by the Byzantine emperor who defeated Chosroes II.

Thus the carpet became yet another casualty of the wars and upheaval that characterize Persia's turbulent history over the last 2,500 years. Of course, the rug might never have existed – it may be a fable. Or if it did exist, it may have been much smaller than it is reputed to have been. Its existence or enlargement may be nothing more than charming evidence of the Persian love of a good story, and of embellishment, not only in the design of carpets.

The greatest period in what is known of the history of Persian rugs and carpets was the sixteenth century, when the Safavids ruled. In the western world at that time, by contrast, pile rugs were almost unknown. A few from Turkey were exported through Venice, and some traders from Antwerp imported rugs from the East. But otherwise, it was as late as the nineteenth century before rugs and carpets became popular. It was not long before they were regarded as necessities in the cultured home, rather than as extraordinary luxuries.

RIGHT An antique silk prayer rug from Tabriz, this piece is "read" from one end only. Prayer rugs very often have an archway framing the top.

24

RIGHT A man from the Kashgai tribe herding his goats on a rocky hillside in the Zagros Mountains in southern Iran.

The acquisition of the Ardebil Carpet for £2,500 by a European museum at the end of the nineteenth century, with the support of ordinary people, reflected the resurgence of interest in Persian rugs in the West. This was encouraged by an exhibition of Persian rugs in Vienna in 1873 and the initiative of merchants in Tabriz, who were the first to supply and respond to the demand by establishing new workshops for making rugs. When they did so, they took inspiration for their designs from elements that can be seen in the Ardebil Carpet and that are typical of Safavid decorative arts, such as flowers and leaves with sinuous interwoven stems and scrolls.

This style is called "curvilinear" and comprises the set of characteristics of classic Persian design most often found on rugs made in workshops and factories from detailed drawings on paper. This continues to coexist in parallel with the rectilinear, which is more typical of tribal rugs, made without drawings on paper, by nomads and by villages in some areas such as around Shiraz.

The lifestyle of Persia's nomadic tribes, and the way that they create rugs, has probably not changed fundamentally in all the many centuries that this brief history of rugs has described. While history was being made all around them, the nomads continued to migrate between summer and winter pastures, tend their herds, and use wool from the flocks' fleeces to make yarn and weave rugs.

This is not to say that the tribes were only ever passive observers to the events of history; on the contrary, their bravery and warriorlike qualities made them attractive participants to rulers who wanted a particular border or coastline protected. From time to time, tribes and portions of tribes were thus transported around Persia for strategic purposes. But once in their new location, the activities of the community continued, including weaving, and of course they brought their existing rugs with them.

This brings us back to the purpose of rugs, and the likely reasons why they first came into existence thousands of years ago. The twice-yearly migration that is the pivot of the nomads' lifestyle makes certain demands upon their living arrangements. Tents and other furnishings must be collapsible and easily transportable. Rugs are clearly suited to this – indeed the fact that you can take them with you when you move is a factor that contributes to their popularity as floorcovering even today.

If you have sheep you generally have wool, and this, of course, is the other obvious reason for the "invention" of the pile rug. Take wool, spin it, weave it into cloth, and at some point someone realizes that you can add pile to it, in imitation of animals' coats perhaps, thereby vastly increasing its comfort and warmth.

Sheep were the nomads' life, their livelihood, and the source of their meat and leather, as they still are today. Sheep provided their wealth, to which rugs (when sold) also contributed. Wool was plentiful and free, and so were various dyes. At the same time, the Persian innate sense of design and decoration found a new and fulfilling outlet. The Persian rug was born.

25

IN A NOMAD'S TENT

OPPOSITE The making of rugs in the nomadic tribes is exclusively the province of the women, who weave kilims, gabbehs, and traditional pile rugs as well as cloths to cover bedding and other possessions piled up at the back of the tent during the daytime (seen here on the left).

THE LIFESTYLE OF THE NOMADIC TRIBES of Iran has not changed dramatically in two thousand years. Some of the trappings are modern — gas-powered stoves for brewing tea in their tents, for example, or plastic sheeting to lay under the rugs on damp ground — but little else has altered. It is still the women who spin, dye, and weave the wool into cloth, kilims, and rugs, in addition to all their other domestic tasks. Twice a year they and their family pack up and make the hard journey, tents, belongings, herds, and all, between the tribe's summer and winter pastures.

Members of the same family make camp in the same valleys and positions that their grandparents and forebears colonized twice a year. The mainstay of their wealth, such as it is, is still the sale for meat of beasts from their herds of wiry sheep and goats, some with bells round their necks, which roam the bare hillsides around their tents in search of grazing.

Among Iran's most distinguished weaving tribes are the Lori, the Afshar, the Balouch, the Kurds, the Shahsavan, and the Kashgai. Other tribes that weave are the Bakhtiar and the Bownat, a subtribe of the Kashgai. The Lori, one of Iran's most significant nomadic tribes, live in the west and south, often adjacent to the Kashgai, whose territory stretches down to the Persian Gulf. Lori rugs are similar to Kashgai ones, and the fringes are often decoratively braided.

ABOVE A painting of tribespeople that is highly romanticized, by Joseph-Austin Banwell.

27

RIGHT The most obvious distinction between townswomen and nomads is the latter's clothing, which is vibrantly colorful and patterned. Here, Kashgai women stand outside the tent observing their menfolk entertain rarely-seen visitors.

The Afshar are a tribe of Turkoman origin with a magnificent history. In the eighteenth century they counted among their members the king of Persia, Nadir Shah. He is famous for defeating the Afghan invaders who had destroyed the court of the Safavid kings, under whom Persian culture had reached its zenith, and for capturing Delhi. From here he took back to Persia the peacock throne. Today, Afshars are famous for their rugs, mostly made by settled members of the tribe. These generally have a cotton warp and weft, use a wide range of colors, and show highly inventive designs, often including birds and animals.

The Balouch tribes traditionally inhabit a large area of eastern Iran. The tribal populations of Afghanistan and Pakistan also largely belong to the Balouch tribe. Their rugs are made in Khorassan, in northeast Iran, and are predominantly sold in the town of Mashad, amongst others. More than almost any other tribe, they produce prayer rugs.

These are small and have a design that includes a squared-off arch. Balouch rugs are generally very finely woven and use a limited number of colors.

The Shahsavan tribe, whose name means "lovers or protectors of the king," traditionally guarded Persia's frontier with Russia and Turkey, one of its most vulnerable borders. They are most famous for weaving kilims made using an unusual technique, known as "soumak" (more about this in detail in Chapter Six: Kilims, starting on page 85).

The Kurds, too, are renowned warriors, with a warlike temperament that has frequently caused trouble, both for them and for others, throughout their history. One of the measures taken to control them was to transport groups to distant parts of Persia. Hence today some live in northwest Iran, others southeast of the Caspian Sea. Their rugs vary according to which group made them; some have cotton warp and weft, some are all wool.

LEFT A colorful Kashgai bag facing, from a bag that would be slung over the back of a donkey or mule during migration.

A rug made by Kurds is often given a name in two parts, such as Kurdi Gouchan. This indicates that it is Kurdish (Kurdi), and has been sold through the town of Gouchan, because the Kurds who made this particular piece are those who live in this area rather than one of the other parts of Iran where Kurds live.

Most tribes in Iran today have members who are settled; that's to say they no longer live in tents and migrate but live in houses in towns and villages. Rugs that carry the tribal name may therefore have been made either by nomads or by their settled sisters. This is certainly true of Bakhtiar rugs. Some are made by nomads in the Zagros mountains west of Isphahan in central Iran, but more are made in the villages in that area.

Nomadic Bakhtiars also make bags of the type in which nomads of all tribes keep and transport their possessions. Bags intended for beasts of burden have areas of kilim and other areas with pile, where the bag leans against the animal, so that the animal is protected from becoming sore. The pile also prevents that part of the bag wearing away too quickly. Bakhtiar rugs are frequently 6 x 10 feet in size, and many are larger. They often use the garden design, in which the rug is divided into compartments, with large blocks of color heavily outlined. The color is known for being especially harmonious, as the tribe generally uses locally-made vegetable dyes.

The Kashgai are the largest of Iran's nomadic tribes. They are also probably the best known, and their rugs are generally of excellent quality in both construction and design. They are famous for their love of color. Believed to have come

ABOVE In this illustration of a camp scene by Nizami from the sixteenth century, the rugs and tents are equally interesting. This appears in "Kamsa," a famous book of poetry.

RIGHT This runner, with its muted warm colors and harmonious floral design, is typical of the Kashgai tribe.

ABOVE An illustration by Rashid Al-Din from a Persian text, showing Genghis Khan seated on a rug inside a tent.

originally from the Caucasus, they now live in southern Iran. Many have settled in villages surrounding the town of Shiraz. They weave several different styles of rug, one result of which is that their rugs are often confused with others made by tribes such as the Kamseh and Lori. They have many subtribes, perhaps the most famous of whom are the Kashguli, who produce carpets that are very finely woven and often show a prayer arch framed by cypress trees.

The landscapes that the nomads inhabit have generally changed little, if at all, over the centuries. Even with its vast twentieth-century cities and petrochemical industries, Iran is a sufficiently huge country geographically (it is very roughly twice the size of France or Texas) to embrace the population increases of the last two millennia without difficulty. Whether this will be the case in the future (the population of Iran has been predicted to double every eighteen years at the current rate) remains to be seen.

Dawn breaks over the Zagros Mountains north of Shiraz, in southern Iran, where the Kashgai tribe make their summer quarters, lighting up the crisply chiseled sandy hills whose appearance is unchanged from Biblical times. Of all the rug-weaving tribes, the Kashgai are among the most accomplished and prolific.

To encounter these nomads, to visit their tents in the Zagros (or at their winter pastures near the Persian Gulf) and glimpse their lives and work, is a chastening as well as a fascinating experience. The directness and dignity with which they welcome visitors (who are indeed rare and themselves a

RIGHT A Turkish bazaar scene painted by Fabius Brest at the end of the nineteenth century. Rugs from Persia were largely imported to the west through Turkey, where much of the buying and selling took place.

source of interest) overcome cultural barriers. An interpreter is often tackling more than just language differences, and these are themselves not to be underestimated since the Kashgai speak a dialect of Turkish, having originated from the Persian border with that country.

There is no difficulty discussing rugs, however. Kashgai women are happy to show off their work, and talk about the creation of individual pieces and their own approach to their weaving. Their culture may not by tradition celebrate the achievements of the individual craftswoman, which is one reason why so few rugs are signed, but the women themselves are not embarrassed to tell you about their work.

In the nomads' tents there is a hierarchy of ground covering. Next to the ground (often with plastic sheeting beneath, depending on conditions) lies a felt rug, either a flat one with a central pattern and border in imitation of a pile rug's design, or a woven one made from inch-wide strips of

felt (the warmer and better insulated option). These felt rugs are bought ready-made in town bazaars and add warmth as well as protecting the pile rugs from the ground below.

On top of this felt layer lie rugs with pile, made in the family and arranged to cover the floor space inside the tent and make it comfortable, rather than with any thought of visual harmony. In the tent of a talented weaving family where each piece is of good quality, the effect is startling. Styles, patterns, and colors jostle for attention. Traditional Kashgai designs in deep rich colors are placed alongside bright new gabbehs (the deep-piled rugs that the tribes traditionally made "for their feet only") and boldly patterned old gabbehs. Some of these have zigzag patterns that are reminiscent of art deco designs.

In a Western home a fine tribal rug or gabbeh tends to take a central position, or rugs are arranged around the floor of a room with others of compatible color and style. Here, the juxtaposition of colors and patterns creates a friction that can

31

OPPOSITE The floor of this tent is furnished with several rugs, topped by a vibrantly colored traditional gabbeh, which will have been woven by the tribeswoman herself, or her daughters. A rug of this boldness and brightness rarely if ever reaches the Western market because agents and dealers do not perceive this as being what customers want.

LEFT AND BELOW Though flamboyant in their choice of color and pattern, Kashgai tribeswomen (left) dress modestly, covering their limbs and hair. This cheerful tribesman (below) wears the traditional gray felt hat with turned-up brim. When it is worn out, his sweater is likely to be unraveled and the yarn incorporated into a piece of woven flooring.

be electrifying. Audiences in drab, postwar Britain must have felt this effect when the Ballets Russes burst upon them. Then, the designs of Leon Bakst, a riot of brilliant color and bold geometric pattern, were considered shocking as well as invigorating. In the same way, the interior of a contemporary Kashgai tent is an antidote to contemporary minimalism.

There is in the Kashgai character a love of pattern, an instinct to decorate, which is nowhere more apparent than in the women's choice of clothes. Whereas the streets of Shiraz (the nearest city) and the surrounding villages are populated by women dressed entirely in black, their hooded forms reminiscent of so many crows, Kashgai women are birds of paradise, plumed in jewel-like colors.

They wear layers of skirts and a long, tabardlike overdress of plain color, patterned color (sometimes more than one pattern in an outfit), glittering color . . . and a scarf over their head to crown the illusion. The older women even color their hair bright orange with henna when it turns gray or white, which adds to the effect of glorious color. Only when she is in mourning does a Kashgai woman dress herself in black.

The men, in contrast, wear relatively drab clothes of brown, gray, black, and blue, long trousers and long-sleeved shirt topped with a jacket or a machine-made patterned sweater. The latter, when it comes to the end of its usefulness as a garment, is likely to be unraveled and recycled, incorporated into a forthcoming rug.

LEFT AND RIGHT These two rugs are both magnificent examples of the work produced by the Kashgai tribe. On the left is an older pile rug in superb condition, with vibrant color such as would rarely be found in a modern piece. The kilim (flatweave) strip next to the fringe at each end is notable. On the right is a newer kilim. The selvage on both pieces is characteristically bound in two colors.

RIGHT A nomad's tent is constructed from strips of goats'-hair cloth sewn together to form a huge sheet, supported by poplar posts. In summer, one long side of the tent is open.

A gabbeh (see page 79), and sometimes a tribal rug, which has areas of color obviously created by chemical dyes, often on man-made fiber, may well have the remnants of a man's or child's sweater woven into it. Such a rug is unlikely to reach the Western market, unless the acrylic color responds well to treatment at the washing factory (more about this in Chapter Four: Color, starting on page 53). On his head an older Kashgai man wears a gray felt hat, which has a domed crown with brim turned up against its sides.

Back in the tent, bedding, clothing, and other possessions not required during the day are piled up across the back of the space to create a flat-fronted "wall" about 4 to 5 feet high and almost as deep. Over this is draped a cloth of some sort, usually a jajim (a homemade woven woolen cloth with plaidlike pattern), or a kilim. Honored guests (or family, in their absence) remove their shoes as they enter the tent, walk on the rugs, and sit with their back to the kilim-covered rampart, supported by rectangular cushions or pillows, to receive small glass cups of tea, drunk without milk but with pieces of sugar served separately for dipping.

Possessions needed during the day and foodstuffs are piled at one end of the tent, the smaller items gathered together in boxes and small, colorful painted tin trunks. Indoor meals are eaten in the central area of the floor, sitting on the rugs, on which are laid a plastic cloth. Some town dwellers in Iran often eat in this manner too, sitting on the floor on a rug.

The tent's opening and sometimes parts of the interior may be decorated with strings of large tassels, some of them brightly colored. These are made by the women with yarn left over from weaving rugs. The weaver makes a strip of wool, along which at fairly regular intervals she introduces a chunky tassel, 6 to 8 inches long. Suspended across the tent's opening, these dance in the slightest breeze.

Kilims are used at night. The pile of bedding that has been stored at the back of the tent during the day is dismantled. Futonlike mattresses and pillows (probably covered with printed floral fabric) are laid out on the floor of the tent, on top of which are laid quilts and, finally, kilims. Layers of rug below and covers above, including the kilim, provide ample warmth and insulation for the night's sleep. Kilims are also sometimes used as "walls," dividing off areas of the tent for privacy.

The quality of design and execution of the rugs in a Kashgai tent varies greatly, depending on the refinement of the weaver as a dyer, designer, and craftswoman. Only the most superior find their way onto the market, especially the export market, and the best of these are superb pieces of work. When she marries, which may be at any age between fifteen and thirty, a Kashgai woman takes some of her weavings with her as part of her dowry, leaving the rest for the family's use (for which they were made in the first place). She might start a new and perhaps different piece to mark the occasion. By the age of thirty she might have sold five or six rugs.

When she marries seems to depend as much on luck as on the woman's personal charms or skill as a weaver. There are few community occasions at which to meet people outside the

LEFT A contemporary gabbeh. There are no traditional design constraints on the weaver, who can follow her instinct in her use of color and portrayal of people, plants, and animals. Gabbehs often have strong abrashes – the marked change of color in the field – which are the result of the wool being hand spun and are part of a gabbeh's charm.

37

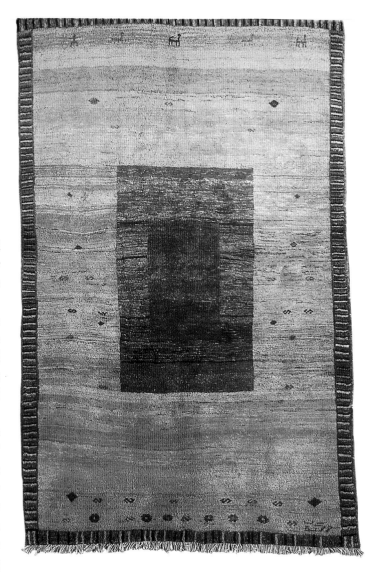

RIGHT Another modern gabbeh, this one with a strong yellow ground and playful striped border.

family – weddings are the only social gatherings of size – and it is strictly up to the man to court the woman. Many marriages are arranged, in which case they depend upon the woman's parents' powers of organization and tenacity.

Nomads' tents are scattered not only over a wide geographic area in any one season, but even within a single valley the tents of relatives within the family are placed individually up the hillside. There is no arrangement of tents with a central communal area along the lines of a traditional image of boy scout or Wild West encampments.

The fabric used to construct a traditional tent of the type used by many tribes is itself made by the women, from goats' hair. The goats' hair fibers from which this cloth is woven have the essential property of swelling in damp weather, primarily rain, so that its loose weave, ideal for ventilation in hot, dry weather, closes up, keeping the tent's inhabitants dry. Woven in a long strip, this goats' hair fabric is joined with other strips to form the roof of the rectangular tent, the joins running horizontally and the covering hanging down on three sides.

The fourth side – a long side in summer and a short one in winter – is left open and generally faces north, the flap forming a canopy. The roof thus formed is supported on slender poplar poles placed upright on the ground. The poles are secured with ropes – also homemade – tied to forked sticks, each of which is secured with the weight of a rock (of which there are always plenty lying around).

If the weaver is working inside the tent for shade, but the rug she is weaving is wider than the gap between the poles (a special commission, perhaps), she rigs up her loom with a pole between two warp threads. The poles are not dug into the ground – they only rest upon it – so it is easy to lift the pole aside when the time comes to weave that part of the rug. The sight of a tent pole apparently standing in the middle of a half-made rug is a strange one, nonetheless.

The lower part of a nomad's tent is formed from a long fence of reeds, woven together with goats' hair yarn, which makes a trellislike pattern on the sticks. The sharp edges along

the top of the fence are bound with a thin strip of cloth similar
to the roof. From a distance it is difficult to spot a traditional
Kashgai tent, so well do its colors and textures merge with the
landscape around it. The women weave cloth and rugs in the
tent for shade or shelter, or outside the tent in mild weather.

Increasingly, though, the Kashgai choose not to live in
traditional tents. They buy fabric tents from the market or
bazaar, which may be round or square rather than rectangular,
with a flap opening at one point in the circumference. Or they
build "modern" tents from materials such as truck awnings,
made from brightly colored plasticized fabric (with the truck's
company name or motif still clearly visible) supported on
metal poles. Inside, however, the arrangement of rugs, kilims,
and possessions is the same. Ventilation is not as good, and
the tents stand out, of course, rather than blending into the
landscape.

This nomadic way of life, which the Kashgai continue to
pursue into the twenty-first century, is not guaranteed to
survive another few decades, let alone a millennium. Pressure
to settle in houses in towns and villages comes from two
directions simultaneously. It comes from government, but it
also comes from within the tribes themselves.

Their young people, who in former times would have
helped with every aspect of the work of keeping herds,
providing the necessities of life, and weaving rugs, are now
compulsorily educated. Not only do children use their school
work as justification for not doing "chores," but many of them
subsequently go away, either to university and to qualify for
the professions, to pass exams and become teachers or skilled
laborers, or simply to work for money in the towns.

Older Kashgai tribespeople, meanwhile, find themselves
without the help they need to maintain the herds, let alone any
other aspect of nomadic life. Naturally, they find the prospect
of old age in a warm house preferable to infirmity in a drafty

LEFT This charming Persian miniature from the later sixteenth century shows the tea ceremony taking place, apparently in a compound in a garden. What is particularly interesting about this picture is the border, which acts as a frame to the illustration and is reminiscent of the border of a rug.

tent. Old men sit drinking tea and discussing the advantages of contraception, since the justification for having a large family (family labor force) no longer applies. In ten years' time, the pessimistic (or realistic) amongst them say, there will no longer be any nomads in Iran.

The Government, meanwhile, offers tribespeople houses for political reasons. A body of people with no settled home, on the move twice a year, is more unpredictable, less manageable, than the same people with permanent addresses. Their needs, government would say, can better be met if they are settled. Already, tribeswomen routinely go to the towns to give birth, and births, deaths, and marriages must be registered with the authorities. The fact that their lifestyle has changed little over so many centuries shows how far "behind" they are.

There is a long history of the authorities attempting to end the nomadic life. The final Shah, Mohammed Reza Shah, deposed in 1979, was the second generation of his dynasty. The first, Shah Reza Pahlavi, was forced to abdicate in 1941, but not before he had attempted to end the nomadic life by using the armed forces to block their migration routes, among other techniques. The last Shah attempted to improve and increase rug production by establishing workshops for the creation of fine pieces, but this had no benefit for tribal rugs, unless it were to raise the international profile of Persian rugs in general.

In the 1940s, the nomadic tribes were still considered political loose cannons. As A. Cecil Edwards wrote in his famous book *The Persian Carpet* (published in 1953), "These

LEFT The rugs in this tent are the work of just one craftswoman and show the range of types typically made by one weaver: gabbeh in the foreground, kilim in the background, and two traditional Kashgai tribal rugs with knotted pile.

nomad tribes differ in speech, race and tradition, so that rivalries, feuds and sometimes open warfare are a common feature of their existence. They live largely outside the pale of governmental authority, and regard robbery as a manly excitement rather than a crime." However, elsewhere he admits that some tribes are better behaved than others, the Kashgai in particular, who "are also the best weavers" in their region.

This is in contrast with the attitude of earlier rulers to the tribes. In previous centuries they were used as a valuable resource in wartime, moved en masse across the country by rulers who wanted a job done, rather like military regiments. Thus the Kashgai came to be in the south of Iran, moved from near the border with Turkey in the northwest, to protect the coast of the Persian Gulf from Portuguese warships.

How the end of the nomadic life, if it comes, will affect rugs remains to be seen. So far, settled tribeswomen have continued the tradition of weaving, on looms frequently adapted for work in a confined space by being upright rather than lain horizontally on the ground. The wool is no longer theirs, shorn from their own sheep and spun by them. They are less likely to dye the wool themselves for practical reasons. But the designs continue to be drawn from tradition, embellished by their own ideas and instinct for decoration. The greatest threat to this last element perhaps comes from the dilution of the tribe through intermarriage, which will be an inevitable consequence, sooner or later, of settlement in towns.

The likely outcome, in due course, of the disappearance of the nomadic way of life is that true nomadic pieces will become more rare, sought-after, and valuable. New pieces and new styles of weaving may yet emerge, however, rather as the production of vibrant new gabbehs in the last decade of the twentieth century has sprung "from nowhere." There may well be new life in the old rug yet.

MAKING
A TRIBAL RUG

PERSIAN TRIBAL RUGS are a joy to own because their appearance gives endless pleasure and they last a lifetime (or longer).

One of the reasons for the rugs' longevity is that they are so well constructed – the good quality ones, at least – from materials ideally suited to the job. The warp and weft are made from wool or cotton, the pile is made from wool, and the wool from wiry mountain sheep is tough and durable, like the sheep themselves. It generally improves with age and a certain amount of friction that comes from use. Indeed, being walked on is considered (not surprisingly perhaps) to be the fulfilling purpose of a rug. A stall holder in the Tehran bazaar will spread a rug out in the alley for an interested customer's inspection; other shoppers walk across it without anyone noticing or thinking this unusual.

Good quality tribal rugs continue to be a pleasure to look at for so many years because they are completely handmade by craftswomen who are technically skilled, have an innate sense of pattern and color, and are practicing a rich tradition that goes back probably thousands of years.

The most obvious way to tell whether a rug has been made by hand or machine is to look at the back. If it is genuinely handmade, the pattern should be as clear on the back as the front – sometimes clearer, if the rug is old and the wool has faded on the front of the pile. There are different ways

OPPOSITE The rich colors and variety of patterns make a pile of tribal rugs and other weavings an attractive sight.

ABOVE A typical Veramin rug showing the Shah Abbasi design in striking reds, blues, and whites on a dark blue ground.

43

LEFT The tribeswoman's loom consists of warp threads attached to two logs of wood laid out on the sandy ground and pinned down with iron loops.

of making rugs by machine. In some cases, the pattern is visible on the back, but in general machine-made rugs do not have a pattern on the back. The pile also looks machine-made, with an irredeemably regular, mechanical perfection.

There is a certain amount of jargon attached to Persian tribal rugs and kilims, as there is to any subject with a technical aspect. Mostly the words simply describe the parts that make up the construction of a piece, and its size. Other words describe aspects of the pattern (see Chapter Five: Rug Patterns, page 69) and color (see Chapter Four: Color, page 53). Knowing the words makes choosing and buying a rug a greater pleasure, as you can then speak the same language as the dealer and find out what he knows about it.

The warp of a rug consists of the threads that run along its length. The weft consists of threads that go from side to side, packing down each row of knots, the tufted ends of which constitute the pile. At the end where the weaver began making the rug there may well be a strip of kilim (a section with no pile) before the pile begins. The Balouch tribe in particular are famous for this; their kilims on pile rugs are often charmingly decorated with embroidery or brocading.

This piece of kilim is next to one of the rug's most vulnerable parts, the fringe. When the fringe on an old rug has worn away or been damaged, the kilim is often unravelled to expose the warps and thus provide yarn for a new fringe. On a rug where there is no kilim, a small strip of the pile border is sometimes unpicked to create a new fringe. This can easily be spotted, and can reduce the rug's aesthetic appeal.

RIGHT This woman is beating down the weft of a new row in her weaving, using a heavy metal comb. As this bounces off the wool it jingles, on account of the metal rings attached to it for decoration.

The fringe is at risk from wear not only by being walked on and scuffed, especially by shoes (nomads remove theirs before walking on rugs), and from being chewed by attentive pets, but most of all from that wonder of modern domestic engineering, the vacuum cleaner. Unknown to people who live in tents without electricity, the vacuum cleaner is the enemy of a rug fringe, which should be brushed away from the rug if it needs cleaning. Fringes on rugs are sometimes knotted or plaited, in which case they are slightly more resistant to damage, especially if they are long. It would not be authentic to plait a fringe that was not made so by the weaver, but this would nonetheless be one way of helping to preserve it.

The other part where the rug is most vulnerable from wear is the selvage, the edges up each side of the rug. Different tribes and weavers have different ways of strengthening the selvage. Some, such as the Kashgai, overweave it with different colored yarn, creating an attractive barber's pole effect (this pattern is often repeated in one of the narrow borders on the rug, known as guardstripes, guardstrips, or guardrails). Others, such as the Balouch, weave a slim band of kilim up each side, sometimes from goats' hair, which gives the design a distinctive brown line on its long sides.

Some rugs have tassels, often brightly colored, at intervals along the selvage. These are generally smart, fat tassels that stand out stiffly from the edge, unlike the large, loose, dangling tassels with which some tribes decorate their tents. They can add a delightful air of festivity to the appearance of a rug, which is enhanced by discovering that this originally denoted a rug that had been made as part of a young woman's dowry. Today, however, it cannot be guaranteed that this is the case, since weavers have realized that tassels are considered appealing and can contribute to a rug's chance of selling.

People selling rugs often refer to the type of knot from which the pile is formed. The two usual types in rugs of good

quality are known as Turkish and Persian (also known as Ghiordes and Senneh). Both are constructed by the weaver manipulating a piece of yarn and two weft threads. A tribe tends to use one or the other (the Kashgai use the Turkish, the Balouch the Persian), but there are exceptions.

To make a Persian knot, the weaver pushes a piece of yarn behind one weft thread, up and over the next thread, then back up between the two wefts. A Turkish knot is made by pushing the yarn down between the two warp threads, up beside one, over both, and back up through the middle. If two warp threads are used in place of each one described above, the knots are called Turkish jufti or Persian jufti. Jufti knots obviously use less wool to make the rug more quickly, so that the rug is rarely of good quality.

Dealers sometimes refer to the number of warp threads and knots per square inch, the greater the number denoting a finer rug. This need not be a real concern, however, so long as you are satisfied that the pile of the rug you like is thick and tight. More important than the exact number of knots is the fact of whether or not you like the design.

Neither Persian nor Turkish knots are actually knots as we think of them – that's to say a secure fastening formed by binding together one or two strings with themselves. It is initially the tautness of the warp, and subsequently the firmness with which the weft thread is beaten back against the knots, which secure the tufts of the pile. Likewise, the design on the pile is not woven but knotted, though the word "woven" is nonetheless generally used of pile rugs as well as kilims.

Warps are made of wool or cotton, according to the tribe's preference and tradition. The Kashgai, who have a supply of wool from their sheep, naturally use wool for wefts. Tribal rugs traditionally have woolen warps, as did many village rugs until recently. Weft threads are wool or cotton and there are generally one or two, sometimes three, of them in a good quality rug. A ruse for making a rug quickly (comparable to the jufti knots) is to use four or more weft threads.

The pile of a tribal rug is invariably made of wool, except where the weaver has become enamored of, or experimented with, acrylic fibers, usually because of their bright color and consequent decorating potential. Rugs with acrylic areas do not usually reach the West because they are not perceived by dealers as being saleable. Some rugs are made with silk pile, but these are a tiny proportion and are made in carefully controlled workshops in the cities, because of the great value of the raw materials and the fineness and accuracy required in their design and execution.

Nomad weavers make their rugs on looms laid on the ground. The loom itself is simply two pieces of wood, tied at the corners and pegged into the ground to secure it. Sometimes the warp threads, having been wound around the top bar of the loom, are gathered into a single knot that is secured to the ground with an iron ring. In either case, the loom can easily be removed, rolled or folded, and transported by animal or truck when the time comes for migration. As she works, the weaver sits on the part of the rug that she has finished, usually on a cloth to protect it.

RIGHT Some tribespeople
and other weavers dye
their own wool; others
buy yarn ready-dyed
from agents or stalls like
this one in the bazaar in
Tehran.

LEFT A small rug, which may have been woven by the Kashgai or by a weaver in or near Shiraz in southern Iran. The tassels may possibly denote a dowry piece, or they may simply have been added for extra decoration.

This contrasts with the loom in a workshop, which is upright and permanent. The weaver sits on a bench that is at least the width of the loom, and which can be raised up in height (it may simply be a board on pegs) as work progresses. Balls of colored yarn are tied to the loom for convenience. Nomads who have settled in villages may weave on the ground, if they can find space, or they adapt to town ways and adopt the upright loom, which makes better sense in an environment where space is at a premium.

Another difference between workshop and tribal rugs is that the former are created from a detailed design drawn on squared paper, which the weaver copies. In some workshops the knots and colors are called out so that a team of weavers can work on the same design in unison. Tribal weavers, by contrast, do not work from a design but use their imagination.

The quality of a rug made by a gifted weaver from one of the nomadic tribes is thus immediately apparent, because there are no textbooks or designs on paper to enable a mediocre craftswoman to disguise her lack of talent. The fact that the design on a tribal rug is "freehand" adds to its charm rather than detracting from it. The occasional eccentricities, where the weaver has had to make an adjustment to her design or has changed her mind about a detail, are appealing because they give you a sense of this piece having been created through the labor of a person with inconsistencies like ourselves, rather than by some anonymous mechanical (or human) agency.

A weaver can only make rugs as large as the loom, which for the nomadic tribes means a size of loom that can easily be transported. A village or workshop weaver can work on a larger loom, making correspondingly larger rugs. One can assume, therefore, that a rug larger than about 5 x 8 feet is not likely to be a genuine tribal piece, although it may have been made by settled tribespeople who have given up the nomadic way of life.

RIGHT Tribal rugs differ in production from those made in workshops in the towns. Here, the weavers (who may be men or women) sit on a bench in front of the loom, which stands in an upright position with balls of yarn hanging above for easy access. The design is drawn up and pinned to the loom – the weavers copy it carefully, producing a finely detailed pattern.

Once the loom has been assembled, the weaver can begin work. First, several rows of flatweave or kilim are woven to strengthen the end of the rug. If this section is wide enough, it is sometimes decorated with a pattern. Then the first row of knots is put in place, the ends of each piece of yarn being trimmed to roughly the final length, before a weft thread is passed across by hand and beaten down against the knots with a large, heavy comb with flat metal teeth. This is done with some force, the comb bouncing off the weft and, if it has rings attached to it, as the Kashgai do for decoration and amusement, it jingles merrily as it bounces.

When she starts a rug, a good weaver has the entire design in her mind; she does not make it up as she goes along. Each rug is a considerable undertaking, and she takes it seriously. Even so, a skilled weaver delights in the work and its quality, and her enjoyment shows in the end result. A rug that makes you smile when you look at it was made with pride and pleasure as well as with skill. After she has finished a small section of the design, she will measure it to check that the finished piece will conform to the category of size she intended.

To the unaccustomed eye, the rugs stacked up in a neat pile in a shop or warehouse look large, medium, or small. Each rug, however, is carefully made to be one type or another, each type having a traditional Persian name. Even the tribal rugs conform to these sizes. The smallest is called a Pushti (or "mat") and is intended to face the cushions against which you sit when talking or eating in a nomad's tent. Next come

LEFT Kilims are carefully folded and piled in a Tehran warehouse awaiting inspection by dealers. An agent or dealer will look at hundreds of rugs or kilims, selecting the occasional item he likes.

FAR LEFT These smaller pieces originally had a variety of uses: as bags, prayer mats, or food coverings. Today they may be enjoyed simply as small wall hangings.

sizes that include the Zarcharak (about 4 x 2½ feet).

The most frequent sizes of tribal rug are the Zaronim (very roughly 5 x 3 feet) and the Dozar (very roughly 6 x 5 feet). These latter two names are easier to remember if you know that "zar" represents approximately 1 meter. "Zaronim" thus means 1.5 meters (or yards) - while "dozar" means 2 meters (or yards). Larger still is the kellegi or keley, which is generally between 11½ and 24½ feet long and 5¾ and 8¼ feet wide. The term "carpet" rather than rug is used to describe large rugs, generally larger than 40 square feet in area.

Rugs are rarely exactly these sizes; rather they are approximations that help to streamline the rug trade so that everyone knows what is being referred to. Interestingly, these sizes are a relatively new "invention," dating from the burst of renewed interest in Persian and oriental rugs that the Western countries demonstrated in the later nineteenth century. Until this time, most Persian rugs were kellegis. This name refers to

the rug's position in the traditional Persian arrangement of rugs on the floor of the main or reception room. This was usually rectangular, with one rug across one end of the room (the head, or keley) and two long, narrow ones down the rest of the length of the room. In a large room there would be three long rugs, two of them narrow, laid down the edges, and another, long rectangular one in the middle.

When a rug is finished, including cutting it away from the loom and neatening or plaiting the fringes, the surface is trimmed. This is a job done with great care, as a mistake could be costly as well as distressing. Some rugs are sold without having first been trimmed, in which case they are finished by machine in the washing factory.

In general, though, tribal rugs are finished and used by the weaver and her family, before being sold, if indeed they ever are. These are, after all, the family's furnishings. A local agent will occasionally arrive and ask if the family has rugs for sale.

LEFT A stack of bundled rugs awaiting attention in a washing factory outside Tehran. These rugs and kilims were selected the previous day in the bazaar in Shiraz by British buyers; now they will undergo rigorous cleaning before being exported to England.

For a foreign tourist, or indeed a city-dwelling Iranian, to ask to buy a rug when shown the inside of a nomad's tent would be rather like having a guest in your home point at one of your possessions and try to persuade you to sell it for cash, while sitting drinking your tea.

Dealers use the (to the layman) comic term "semi-old" to describe rugs of a certain age. This means that they guess the rug to be between twenty and fifty years old, during which time it will have been furnishing a nomad's tent. If the rug is newer it is called "new," older and it is called "old." Naturally, being in a nomad's tent results in some wear. Some rugs actually have holes in them, which are mended at the washing factory before the rug is offered for sale. Others are simply worn in patches, which in time may meet right across the rug. It is testament to tribal rugs' superb construction that a rug can be almost bald, yet not only is the pattern still completely visible, but the patina on the surface is glossy and the piece is still beautiful, and indeed usable if it is not too valuable.

C O L O R

OPPOSITE Gabbehs are characterized by strong hues and spontaneous designs: here ocher, vermilion, and cobalt blue – the colors of earth and sky – combine in simple geometric shapes.

WHATEVER YOUR COLOR SCHEME — neutrals, primaries, or rich jewel-like tones — there is a rug or kilim that will not only complement it, but will also make a positive contribution to the appearance of a room. Rugs are made in every color that can be created by dyeing wool, from the soft browns and pinks of the Afghan kilim to the rich reds and blues of traditional Persian tribal knotted rugs. There are the bright kilims whose tones and bold geometric patterns are at home with brilliant contemporary colors. And then there is the gabbeh, a type of rug that is uniquely modern in many ways, including its use of color (more about gabbehs in Chapter 5: Rug Patterns).

The colors of all these different types of rug, the richness and variety of their tones, are their most immediate charm. The colors sing out to us, communicating in a way that is direct, primitive, and seductive. But the rugs in our homes are not only beautiful in themselves; they are the culmination of a magnificent history of skill in using color and pattern in weaving.

Color is a fundamental part of the nomadic weavers' creations, and of their rug's or kilim's appeal. Traditionally, the colors at their disposal were not huge in range, depending upon the available dyes, but they were rich in tone. The weaver's great skill was in balancing the available colors and combining them in a satisfying composition.

ABOVE Perhaps the most appealing aspect of this gabbeh is its charming border showing animals and trees.

LEFT AND BELOW Rugs being scrubbed inside a washing factory (above) before being taken outside to dry (below), some laid on pebbles on the ground, some hung over poles.

It is interesting to discover, therefore, that these colors we admire were not always as we see them. The colors on a rug might well have been quite different when the rug was being woven. With a rug that is fifty or a hundred years old, this is not so surprising. You would expect the harsh sunlight of the Middle East to bleach color from almost any material over a period of time.

But the colors of modern rugs, too, have been altered. Before being exported, rugs of all ages go through a thorough process of washing, sunning, mending, and any other adjustments that the agent or dealer feels are necessary to bring the rug to the height of its beauty before it is dispatched to the discerning collector abroad. Some, after all, will have been on the floor of a nomad's tent for several years, decades even, being walked on (albeit without shoes) and having the dust of the sandy hillside trodden into them.

The preparation process is in five parts. Firstly, the rug is beaten in a machine to remove the bulk of the dust and dirt. If there is an unacceptable amount of fluff on the back of the rug, this is singed off with a giant blowtorch. Any bad holes are stabilized with a few large stitches to prevent them from becoming worse during washing.

Secondly, the rug is washed with water and a solution of calcium hypochlorite to give the colors a slight golden glow, before it is rinsed and dried in the sun. The washing takes place on a sloping concrete floor with water faucets along the upper edge. The rugs are scrubbed by men each holding a "kaj bill," a long-handled tool with a flat metal head used to rake

LEFT AND RIGHT The final stages of preparation before a rug or kilim is ready for export: cleaning small remaining blemishes (left, above), mending (left, below), and painting areas where the blue has faded unacceptably (right).

the pile vigorously up and down while at the same time they walk on it in rubber boots.

The third step is to send the rug to a remote place such as the town of Yazd, where it lies for up to three months, its colors softening in the sunlight. Then it returns to the washing factory for the fourth stage, another thorough wash. This time shampoo is used, as well as chemical solutions that soften the wool, reduce any garish colors, and give the pile added shine. The rug is then treated with conditioner and rinsed, before being spun in a "hydro extractor" (otherwise known as an industrial spin dryer) and dried in the sun again.

Once you have seen the treatment to which rugs are subjected in a washing factory, you appreciate what superbly hardwearing objects they are. Any apprehension you might have had about cleaning the occasional spill or mark on your rug disappears (though it is always important to use only gentle chemicals for spot-cleaning, definitely not bleach).

The yard of a washing factory is a fine sight, with acres of rugs lying on pebbles to dry, or hung on rails around the edge. A huge beating machine, 20 feet high, dominates one corner, while in another a group of men sit, mending rugs that have holes or damaged fringes. This and any color retouching is the final stage of preparing the rug for sale.

Color retouching is known as "painting" and involves the workman literally painting color back into a rug where dark blue colors have faded dramatically, upsetting the balance of tones in the rug's design. Painting is considered a normal part of preparing a rug for sale in the wider market and does not detract from its value – rather the opposite, in fact, since its appearance is improved. Besides blue, the color most frequently painted is bright orange, which is toned down with strong tea.

There are ways of checking whether a rug has been painted. A skillful painter paints only to the edge of the color he is

LEFT A woman from the Kashgai tribe and her daughter. The woman is spinning wool using a traditional spindle, which she keeps in her pocket ready for use whenever her hands are idle.

retouching; a less skillful one misses slightly here and there, which can easily be seen with careful inspection. The bottom of the pile can be revealing: if blue areas have been painted, the fibers near to the warp and weft will be a shade of dark gray, while the back in these areas will probably still be dark blue. Another test is simply to spit on your finger and rub the pile: a bluish shadow will appear on your finger if the pile has been painted.

The story of color in rugs begins, of course, with the wool itself. In June the sheep are taken to the river for a preliminary wash and are then shorn. The wool is washed again, carded, and spun. The Kashgai women use a spindle that has a central metal stalk, from which protrude four curved, black plastic prongs, pointing upwards and reminiscent of the small animal horns which, together with wood, was what the spindle was originally made from. If she is not doing anything else, a woman will take her spindle out of her pocket and spin as she stands, walks, or sits. Spinning is a constant background activity for Kashgai women.

Wool is sorted into yarn for warp and weft threads on the one hand, and yarn for knotting on the other. The latter is then dyed while the other is left its natural cream, gray, or brown. Some tribes, including the Kashgai, have a tradition of also dyeing the yarn for weft threads. If you look at the back of an old Kashgai rug, you will sometimes find another entire pattern, different from the front, because the weft threads are red or pink, sometimes with alternating irregular stripes of these two, and other, natural colors. Occasionally you will also

COLOR

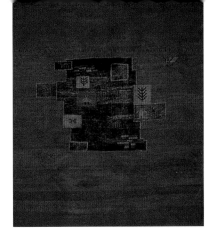

RIGHT A wonderfully free-form gabbeh design on a rich red ground or field. Shades of red are produced by dyeing yarn in runas or cochineal.

BELOW A bowl of dried "jasheir," a feathery-leaved plant that grows in Iran and is used as the main ingredient in dyeing the distinctive egg-yolk yellow yarn used in all types of rugs and kilims.

find blue weft threads, probably in a rug from Kashan and other parts of central Persia.

Dyeing is a huge and fascinating subject in itself. Today, various types of both natural and chemical dyes are used to color the wool for rugs. The aim is to produce yarn of the most desirable colors, and while some natural dyes continue to be used because they are readily available and effective, other less effective ones have been replaced by chemical dyes that are more reliable, colorfast, and do not rot or otherwise damage the yarn.

The history of dyes can give clues to the date of a rug. Indigo, for example, is a historic dye that features in ancient African legends and is believed to have been one of the ingredients in the blue woad that barbaric Britons used to decorate themselves, with the intention of terrifying the enemy in battle. Almost everywhere in the world it was found, however, indigo was a revered and relatively rare ingredient.

The Persian people were able to cultivate the *Indigofera* plant in a few areas and produce a small amount of indigo dye. Otherwise, it was imported from India. Blue, its beauty enhanced by its rarity and value, became one of the central colors of tribal weavers' designs. Indigo's tendency to fade was to a certain extent part of its perceived charm. Today, by contrast, synthetic indigo dye, chemically identical to the original, is easily available and the popularity of the color blue has, if anything, increased.

Weavers and workshops understand that blue is an appealing color to those of us who are the rugs' ultimate

customers. Blue is therefore used freely in contemporary rugs, which are known as "new production." The blue is no less beautiful because it is created by a synthetic dye; on the contrary, it is not the dyestuff that gives the wool its beauty, or even the fact that it has been dyed by hand.

The element that gives the wool used to make Persian tribal rugs its wonderful depth and variety is the fact that it has been carded and spun by hand. This means that the yarn is not perfectly even in thickness, even when it appears so to the naked eye. When the yarn is dyed, the finished color is correspondingly slightly uneven, with tiny subtle variations that cause it to "sing" to the human eye, making it ever a pleasure to look at. This quality is unaffected by the method of dyeing, be it by an individual tribeswoman, by men in an outdoor factory, or by machine. In all these cases, the dye and the fibers of the wool form a chemical bond (providing the dye is administered correctly), which prevents the color from washing out. This is the difference between a dye and a stain, which is potentially fugitive.

Occasionally a rug includes areas of color created by machine-dyed wool or acrylic fibers in garish colors. These are more than distinctive – they leap out at you – and such a rug is extremely unlikely to be chosen by an agent or dealer for export from Iran, even if (and this is rare indeed, but not unknown) the acrylic adds a dash of brilliance or humour to an otherwise sober composition. The dealer would simply be taking too great a risk. Hand-dyed wool is preferred because it has subtle variations that give life to the surface of the pile

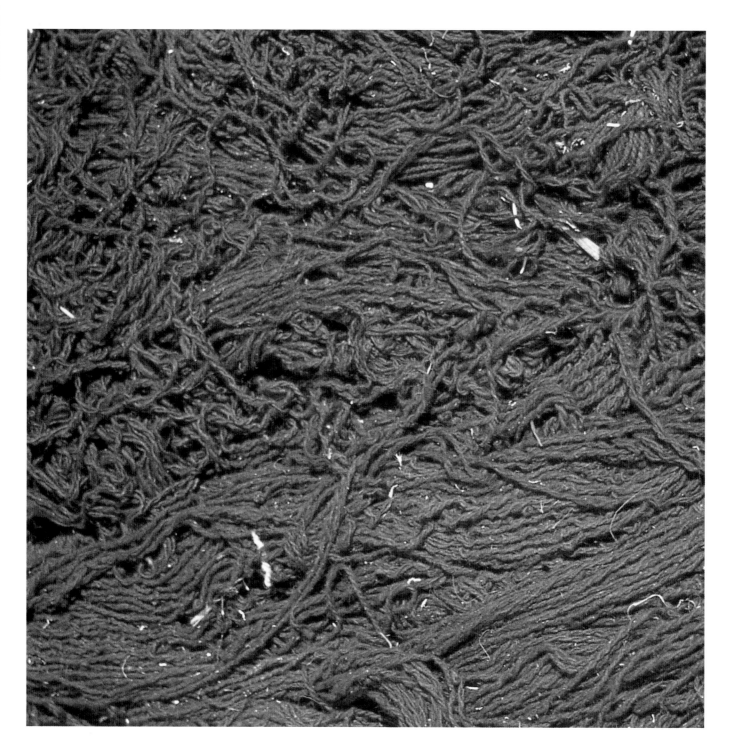

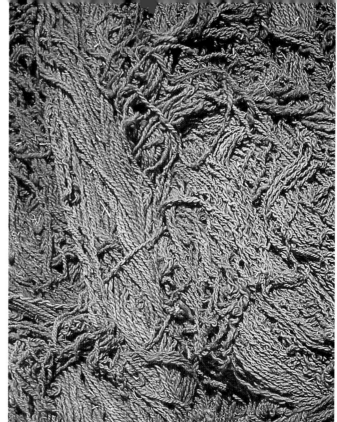

even when the rug appears at first glance to have a field of flat color.

The principal colors that are still made using natural dyes are reds of all hues and yellows. Shades of red are drawn from two separate ingredients, the madder plant (known locally as "runas") and small female beetles of the *Coccus cacti* (cochineal) family. To make dye from the madder plant, the root is dug up in October or November, when it is between three and nine years old (the older the plant, the darker the red). The root is then dried, ground, and boiled, and the resulting color can be a purplish-red like wine, or it can veer towards orange.

Cochineal, like indigo, was once imported from India and used almost exclusively in eastern Iran. In western Iran the weavers tended to use the madder plant because it grew wild and was thus freely available, and free. The use of cochineal is fairly widespread today, however, and the dye is mainly imported from Mexico.

Women in the tribes still dye a certain amount of yarn themselves. They make or buy the dyes, then boil the yarn in them, having first soaked it in a mordant (or having added mordant to the dye), which enables the dye to adhere to the wool fibers. The final color of the yarn is influenced by a number of factors that will never all be exactly the same twice: the age of the dye plant (or concentration of dye), the type and intensity of the mordant, the hardness of the water, its temperature and the container in which it is heated, and the relative oiliness of the wool.

Chemical dyes have been welcomed to replace certain natural dyes that actually harmed the wool – oak galls, for example, used to make black and brown, contain salts that cause the woolen fibers to wear rapidly. Other natural dyes such as the yellow drawn from saffron were known to fade.

There are various reasons, some more valid than others, why natural as opposed to chemical dyes are perceived as being

RIGHT Yarn freshly dyed with imported chemical indigo is draped over the walls of a vat in an outdoor dyeing factory on the outskirts of Shiraz in southern Iran.

OPPOSITE When the dyeing process is complete, the bundles of yarn are laid on the ground in the sun to dry.

desirable. One is that all things natural are seen as eco-friendly (or at least, the Western customer is believed to prefer them); another reason is anthropological – it is a loss to all mankind when human skills disappear, replaced by manufactured goods, especially skills in which man interacts with his environment, as in the knowledge and gathering of dyeing ingredients.

A third reason is historical. Invented by Sir William Henry Perkin, an Englishman, in 1856, the first chemical dyes were accidentally discovered in the quest for a synthetic form of the medicine quinine. Known as aniline dyes, they were bright and inexpensive, and were soon widely used across the world. They proved to be unreliable, however: colors faded dramatically, as can be seen in many a Victorian lady's embroidery.

In the meantime, however, Persian rug makers had adopted aniline dyes with enthusiasm. The reputation of the Persian rug industry (a vital part of the economy) was at stake, and aniline dyes were forbidden in 1903. Anyone who used them risked having an arm amputated or their workshop burnt down. This experience of aniline dyes has not been forgotten, even though modern chromatic chemical dyes are unrelated to their aniline forebears, and are colorfast and reliable. Most handmade rugs are today made from a mixture of wools dyed using natural and chemical ingredients, the best of each.

In order to obtain chemically dyed wool, Kashgai tribes-women either obtain dye from a local bazaar, or they sell yarn and buy ready-dyed wool with the proceeds. They can also supply undyed yarn to an agent, who returns them dyed wool

for a fee (probably their own yarn, since the Kashgai are the major producers of wool in southern Iran). Parcels of yarn, already dyed in various colors, are supplied to settled weavers who are working on commissioned pieces.

Wool that is supplied to the weaver (or bought from a stall of the bazaar) has not necessarily been dyed by machine. Dyeing factories are often low-tech establishments where the main (possibly the only) difference between "home" and "factory" dyeing is the scale of the operation. At a dyeing factory on the outskirts of Shiraz, in the south of Iran, the process is much as it would be outside a Kashgai tent, but on a larger scale.

Here, yarn is immersed in large rectangular vats, each of which requires 1,300 gallons of water for 660 pounds of wool. Each tank has a domed boiler in the base for heating or boiling the wool for anywhere up to seven hours, after which it steeps for up to a further 24 hours (each color has a different recipe).

After dyeing, the bundles of wool tied with colored twine lie on the ground to dry in the sun. The entire process takes place in the open air, all year round, operated by men with the aid of machines such as boilers and hydro extractors. The same dyes are used (some natural, some chemical), and different tones emerge for the same reasons as when the wool is dyed by individuals.

Factories such as this supply wool ready-dyed (naturally and chemically) to retained rug makers in the villages. The worker is paid for his or her labor, and the rug is weighed

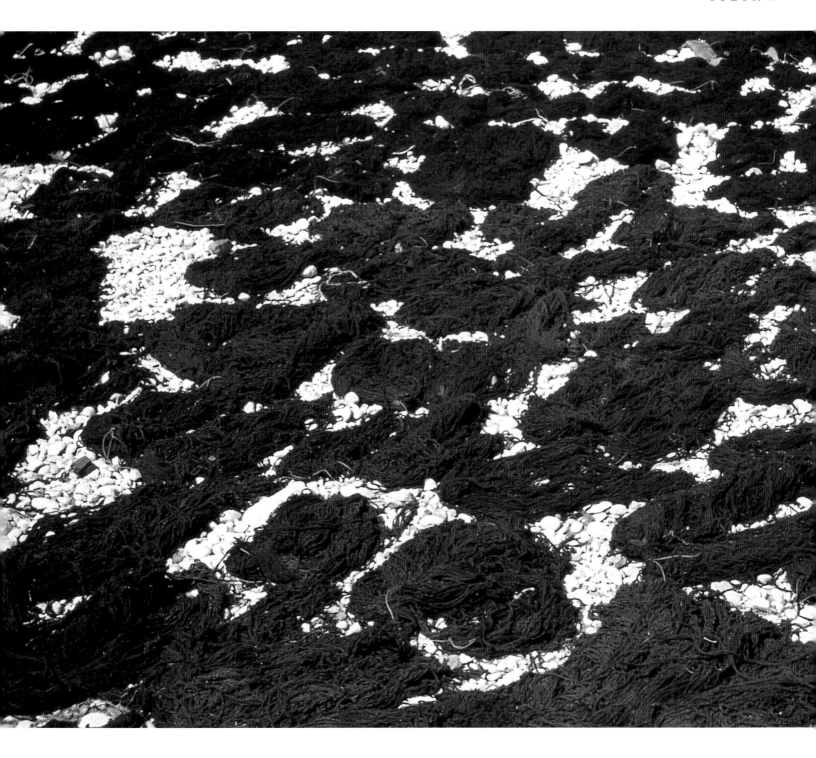

RIGHT A stack of brightly-colored kilims piled up in a warehouse in Shiraz. A visiting buyer specifies what type and size of rug or kilim he is seeking; the warehouse owner knows exactly where these are and instructs his men to bring them out for inspection.

when finished to ensure that it contains an amount of wool equal to that supplied.

Interestingly, while in the tribes it is the women who spin, dye, and weave (in addition, apparently, to doing all the other work except tending the herds), in the villages and town bazaars like Shiraz, weavers are of both sexes, while dyers and the workshop overseers are invariably men.

One of the most appealing results of the yarn having been dyed by hand is the "abrash." This is a streakiness in what would otherwise be a flat area of color, on the field of a rug. The word itself is derived from a Turkish word referring to the dapples on a horse. Some abrashes are hardly visible; others are extremely noticeable. Abrashes are the result of two possible events. Either the weaver has changed from one batch of dyed wool to another whose color is not exactly the same; or it is caused by the batch or skein of yarn being of slightly uneven color.

These subtle changes in color occur in a batch of yarn because, having been spun as well as dyed by hand, the strands are marginally thicker in some places than others, and have consequently absorbed less dye. The varying thickness of the fibers themselves can also be the cause of subtly uneven color in a single skein of yarn, as can the amount of lanolin fat the wool contains, and the extent to which minute air bubbles cling to the fibers during the dyeing process.

Abrashes do not make a tribal rug less valuable – rather the opposite, since they are a reminder of the fact that this is a handmade work of craftsmanship, created by an individual, not a factory. A machine-made rug looks mechanical; a handmade one, especially a tribal piece, has subtle variations of color that breathe life into it, give it added visual interest and character, and contribute to its growing beauty over the years.

One of the ways in which it is possible to identify which tribe has made a rug is its use of color. Kashgai rugs, for

Right A small, old
gabbeh with an unusual
design of stylized
butterflies in rhythmic
rows of three.

Below A colorful Kashgai
kilim, which uses the
familiar segmented
octagon motif found on
many such pieces.

example, have strong, deep colors. The red is particularly beautiful, being a glowing ruby color. Another significant tribe, the Lori, is fond of red, theirs being strong and deep. Balouch rugs also use red (as indeed do all the tribes, the dye being readily available and free), but with more white than most other tribes, usually with strong areas of blue and black or dark brown.

The symbolism and hidden meaning of the colors found in Persian rugs is a perennial source of fascination. Gray, for example, has been described as being the color of secrets and withdrawal (the latter being a not inaccurate description of its effect in a design) while yellow, the color of sunlight, spoke of plenty, riches, power, and the attainment of happiness. Orange was said to evoke tenderness and devotion, purple self-determination and magic.

Though charming and poetic, the significance of color can be a disappointing theme to pursue into the modern world, however. Whatever meaning the colors once had, they are largely lost to the tribes, who choose and use color in their rug designs according only to availability, tradition, and aesthetic considerations. Their instinct is always to decorate, and the increasingly easy availability of dyed yarn is a delight to them, one that overcomes any distant, half-forgotten symbolism.

Green, for example, was the color of the banners of the first Muslim troops, and was therefore too holy to be trodden underfoot, even without shoes. In fact, green is quite often found, albeit generally in small but telling areas.

In decorating terms, the most significant color in a rug is generally that of the ground, the area inside the border and outside the central motif or medallion. The overall tone of a rug that has a detailed design covering the whole field is also important. If you can't decide what this is at a glance, take a step back and screw up your eyes. This should give you a better impression of the overall hue. In tribal rugs reds, rich browns, and blues predominate. These colors obviously complement the mellow color of polished antique furniture and wooden floors, and the patina of well-worn terracotta tiles (see Chapter Seven: Floors, on page 101).

Kilims, by nature of their bold geometric patterns, tend to look as nice in contemporary as in older surroundings, as do gabbehs, which are particularly well suited to modern interiors because of their free-form designs and light, vibrant colors.

DECORATING WITH RUGS & KILIMS

Opposite The bedroom of someone who is passionate about tribal rugs and kilims. The cushions, throws, and rugs add warmth and texture to the room.

RUG PATTERNS

THE SURFACE DESIGN OF A RUG is made up of color and pattern. The patterns of Persian rugs have been a source of fascination for as long as the rugs have been available in the West, and are one of their greatest charms. Most other textile patterning in the home is continuous; that is to say it comes off a roll – fabric for curtains or upholstery, for example. A rug, however, offers pattern in a capsule, with a self-contained design all its own. Tribal rugs, in particular, have designs that are unique since the traditional weaver works free hand, without copying from a drawing or pattern on paper, unlike weavers in town workshops.

Each tribe has a pattern "style" that they produce on their rugs, each style being the combination of a number of elements. As in other art forms, some of these elements are unique to one group, while others appear in the work of more than one. Over the centuries, weavers have absorbed new influences and ideas, and there are now many common design elements. In general, however, they take pride in weaving in the rich tradition of their own family and lineage. Dealers can usually identify a rug's provenance at a single glance.

Although it is not necessary to know all the styles by heart in order to enjoy a tribal rug in one's own home, it is interesting to have some idea of who made your rug, and a little knowledge can make buying a rug or simply visiting a rug warehouse or shop an enriching experience.

Kashgai rugs, for example, typically use red, a rich deep blue, and a yellow that varies in color from pale to golden or ocher. A typical rug has a lively border including zigzags and clearly marked spandrels (the corner sections inside the border), which each contain a sunflower design. In the center is a medallion (or two or three, of equal size, in a line up the middle of the rug) containing a geometric motif known as the "crab" because it approximates the shape of that creature. The field or ground (the area outside the medallion and inside the border and spandrels) is decorated with individual flower motifs and birds. Both warp and weft are wool (as opposed to cotton) and the pile is made with the Turkish (as opposed to the Persian) knot (see page 46).

None of these elements is unique to the Kashgai. The colors are common to a large proportion of traditional tribal weavings, and the crab, flowers, and birds are all to be found in some other rugs. It is the pattern created by a combination

OPPOSITE ABOVE A typical runner from Tafresh, east of Hamadan in northwest Iran.

OPPOSITE BELOW A superb Kashgai rug with lions in the field, around three connected medallions in the center.

LEFT Two rugs drying in the sun. On the left is a typical Lori, with a bold, unfussy design. On the right is a Balouch rug with the Paisley-like boteh motif.

of these colors and motifs in an overall design that makes it possible to identify such a rug as typically Kashgai.

The Lori and Balouch are other important weaving tribes. A typical Lori rug is distinguished by its bold, graphic design. The pattern is not busy, as on some rugs. The ground is a distinctively orange shade of red, and contains geometric shapes. The warp is made of cotton, the weft is wool, and the pile is constructed with Persian knots. These three elements are also typical of a Balouch rug.

A typical Balouch creation contrasts with the Lori on account of its finely-drawn design, which includes the "boteh," a paisley-type fish shape (more about this on page 75). It uses only a few colors, giving an overall impression of warm, rich darkness. The borders are wide in proportion to the size of the rug, and contain much detailed pattern. Distinctively, the selvage (down the edges) is wide and flat, incorporating five warp threads.

A Balouch rug illustrates an interesting point about the appeal of Persian tribal rugs. Its mellow colors, its generous borders, and its geometric design that is at the same time both intricate and spontaneous, make it almost the epitome of the "Persian rug" as we know it. A prosperous Tehran housewife, on the other hand, is unlikely to want such a rug in her home. She would prefer a much more expensive workshop-made rug, thin and smooth, the work astonishingly fine. The design of her ideal rug includes arabesques and flowers described in razor-sharp detail, the colors pale, ideally mauves and pinks on a white ground. If she is aware of the Balouch's or the Kashgai's existence, she is probably not much interested in them. Taste is so much the product of time and place.

Kurdi Gouchan rugs have much in common with Balouch rugs. Made by Kurds who were moved from the west to the eastern borders several hundred years ago, probably for defensive purposes, they too use predominantly rich, dark

LEFT A typical Joshaghan has blocks of pattern in the border, one central medallion, strictly regimented flowers on the field, and the same in the spandrels but on a blue background.

BELOW The largest of these is an Afshar Sirjan with typical medallions and a two-sided castle. Sometimes the castle on a rug of this type has square castellations.

colors and designs with detailed borders. A Kurdi Gouchan rug, however, may well have a quantity of white in the border, which lightens the effect. Green is quite often a third color in the design, in addition to red and black or dark blue.

One of the most poetic of Persian rugs is perhaps the garden design typically made by the Bakhtiar people. The garden has a special place in Moslem thought and for the Persian people as a whole. It is a small piece of paradise, a place where one may rest and revive, a promise of what is to come. Water is significant: a pool of still water provides a reflection of heaven while water running through a channel or a fountain is a source of life, its sound like music in heaven.

A Bakhtiar garden rug might have a field divided into as many as forty separate sections. The borders between the squares or rectangles are pathways or streams; and the squares each contain a tree, flower, or bird. Unlike many other tribes and weaving groups, the Bakhtiar use a wide palette of colors, including pinks, reds, and greens, which bring the surface to life and produce a jewel-like effect. They are renowned for using natural dyes, though occasionally their love of color leads them to use chemical dyes with the result that a flash of orange or turquoise stands out. A Bakhtiar rug typically has a cotton warp with wool weft, and is made using the Persian knot.

A Joshaghan rug is made by settled weavers (who have never been nomads) in a village of that name close to Isphahan in central Iran. The typical Joshaghan design is a delight. Similar to so many rugs including the Kashgai, it divides the

LEFT An old Kashgai rug whose design uses plenty of white and relatively little red, which makes it unusual. More modern pieces usually have more red. The catlike creatures are probably leopards.

73

LEFT A Kashgai rug that is fairly typical of its type, except that it is longer than is usual.

surface into borders, spandrels, medallion, and ground. The border uses blocks of color and has two further, thin borders on each side (known as guardrails or guardstripes) whose designs mirror each other and which use the same green and red. The medallion in the middle of the rug is small in relation to the size of the whole rug, and the ground has regimented rows of stylized flowers, each contained within a diamond or lozenge shape.

The most interesting detail of this rug's design is the spandrels. Here, the field of flowers continues, but the color of the field changes from red to blue. The overall impression the rug gives is of great richness, but the discipline of the regimented rows of flowers in the field gives it a dignified restraint. On other non-Joshaghan rugs the field motifs are often scattered with seeming abandon.

Flower motifs are among the most frequent to appear in Persian tribal rugs, along with the crab, herati (a diamond shape with spokes sticking out of it and a leaf or fish at the end of each spoke) and boteh (paisley-type fish shape). When you have seen the landscape in which the Kashgai, for example, make their spring and summer camp near the town of Shiraz, it is easy to understand why flower motifs are so popular. What looks from a distance like a desert hillside spotted with tufts of scrub is, on closer inspection, host to a great variety of verdant plants, largely thistles and succulents. Their exquisite forms and mass of flowers light up the rocky slopes, give shelter to butterflies and small birds, and provide nectar for the bees that some tribesmen keep in boxlike hives. Towns,

LEFT A charming motif of two birds, so close together that they appear to be kissing like love-birds, from a Kashgai rug.

BELOW The love of flowers was not exclusively Persian. The elaborate, lusciously naturalistic flowers on this rug are typical of Indian pieces of the sixteenth century.

too, have gardens overflowing with roses, geraniums, oleander, hibiscus, and flowering fruit trees, to name but a few.

The boteh is a particularly interesting motif and one that has, over many centuries, crossed the world. No one knows where it began, but it is to be found in Indian textiles and Scottish paisley shawls as well as rugs woven by several nomadic tribes. There are almost endless theories about its meaning and origin. It is variously said to resemble the leaf of the palm tree, a seed, the flame of Zoroaster, an almond, a pear, a leather purse, the course of the river Jumna, and even a fist-print in the blood of an embittered, defeated king. It has been known as the Persian Pine pattern.

The boteh itself appears on rugs in many different guises: as a simple, geometric hexagon with a hook sprouting from the top, as an elegantly curved shape containing flowers or further small botehs, and as an elaborately embellished tear-drop. Where a field is entirely covered with repeated rows of botehs, they usually face in one direction in one row, the opposite way in the next, and so on.

Another important shape and pattern is the gul or octagon, which is sometimes enlarged by extra corners, sometimes shrunk into a diamond shape, usually divided up inside into further small pieces and patterns. The mina khani pattern consists of rosettes surrounded by four other flowers that are linked with arcs. This unit is repeated across the entire field of the rug, most typically in Veramin rugs (see page 92). Rosettes are flowers seen face on, while palmettes are large flowers seen as if drawn from the side in cross-section. The

Above and right Both these rugs incorporate texts. The one above is from Heriz and was made in the nineteenth century. The text is Islamic, while the modern one on the right has a signature cartouche. The design of the modern piece is unusual in that its four quarters are not mirror images; instead, the tendrils or arabesques (the Persian word for these is "eslimi") trail asymmetrically and elegantly from one segment into another.

RIGHT The double-headed horse: on the right is one of the carved figures that once topped a column at Persepolis, the palace-city in southern Iran created by the emperor Darius; on the left is a gabbeh incorporating the horse with two heads, probably made by the Kashgai tribe.

Shah Abbas designs (there is a seemingly endless variety of them) are so called because they use rosettes and palmettes, and sometimes medallions, in a way first formulated in the reign of that supposedly beneficent ruler.

An attractive motif that often appears in Kashgai rugs is the double horse's head. This refers to Persepolis, the fabulous city created by the Persian king Darius. Persepolis is not far from Shiraz, and the Kashgai migration route to their summer pastures can lead them close to it if they are traveling in the direction of Isphahan. All that remains now are some ruins, including many tall stone columns, which would have had the double horses' heads atop them if these had not been destroyed or defaced in the course of the Arab Muslim invasion of Persia in the seventh century AD. These invaders considered the portrayal of men or animals in art as sacrilege.

One of the most intriguing aspects of the pattern of flatweaves, in particular, is their similarity to the patterns on textiles of other cultures. This is true of kilims, jajims, and, to some extent, old gabbehs that have simple geometric designs. Some jajims' patterns are remarkably similar to Scottish tartans or plaid, while some kilims' designs have a distinctly Mexican or Aztec look to them.

While it would be romantic to believe in a cross-pollination of ideas spanning time and space, the reality is probably far more prosaic. Such patterns are the result of the method of production: with a simple rectangular loom and yarn extending in straight lines in two directions, even the most inventive of weavers is likely in due course to create designs that have similarities to textiles made by other weavers with the same type of basic equipment.

The most recently invented patterning on Persian rugs occurs on a particular type of gabbeh. The modern gabbeh is a remarkable phenomenon – an entire type of Persian rug that is new, born in the last decade or so of the twentieth century,

RIGHT Two old gabbehs
that illustrate the
dynamic geometry that
brings so many of these
rugs to life.

out of a combination of factors. Gabbehs have been made
from time immemorial, but the old rugs, which the tribes
described as "for our feet only," look completely different
from the new ones. The colors of the old rugs are rich,
sometimes somber, sometimes muted, based (as in traditional
Persian rugs) on vegetable dyes. New gabbehs are mostly
brightly colored, often abstract and dynamic in design, always
lively, and above all they look completely modern. They take
to the limit that sense of spontaneity that imbues all the best
nomads' rugs and that marks them out as the creations of
individual craftspeople.

What the old rugs have in common with the modern
gabbeh, and the reason why they share the name, is that they
are, or were initially, so-called "recreational" weaving. This
was distinguished from other weaving because they were for
their own entertainment and use, the designs often
experimental, consisting of any motif the weaver found
appealing. The women of the nomadic tribes are supremely
skilled craftspeople, and just as a gifted chef might look
forward to having his kitchen to himself in order to
experiment and have a bit of fun in his time off, so the nomads
continue to weave after the serious pieces have been finished,
but purely for their own pleasure.

Old and new gabbehs also have in common the spontaneity
of their designs. In the case of the old, these are often
geometrical, consisting of abstract zigzags or motifs,
sometimes positively eccentric in their design or arrangement.
Some old gabbehs' designs are closely related to the patterns

LEFT Another small, old gabbeh, this one showing goats and a popular tribal motif, the tree of life.

RIGHT A detail of a gabbeh. The weaver has the entire design in her mind before she starts; here she depicts a woman (herself perhaps), sheep or goats, and a flower motif.

BELOW All contemporary gabbehs are in some sense experimental, since the weavers follow no tradition. This has creatures in the borders rather than roaming free.

on kilims. New gabbehs, however, are completely modern. They show images of anything that takes the weaver's fancy, those reaching the shops in the West often including the human figures, plants, and animals that constitute the weavers' daily lives or fantasies.

The old recreational pieces have been known to carpet buyers visiting the nomads for many years. They would buy a few, but as there was no great demand for them in the West, they were rarely found in the shops of Europe or the Americas. Gabbehs were considered the poor relations of the rug world.

The trigger for the creation of a new school of gabbehs occurred in continental Europe in the 1980s. A fresh generation wanted rugs to decorate their homes, but not rugs in the style that their parents and grandparents owned. A demand arose for a new type of decorative floorcovering, and enterprising weavers and buyers supplied that demand.

Weavers grasped with enthusiasm the opportunity to work with fresh, brilliant colors on the new gabbehs, many of them supplied by modern chemical dyes. In creating gabbehs, not only were the weavers free from the traditions of color that were based on their ancestors' ability to produce mellow reds, blues, and yellows from natural ingredients, but their designs could also roam freely across the rug, unfettered by tradition.

Gradually other markets were persuaded to overcome their suspicions that gabbehs were too primitive or avant garde. Within a few years the popularity of the new-style gabbehs boomed, to the extent that dealers feared that the demand was deceptive and could not last.

RIGHT A traditional gabbeh with a bold and contemporary design. This one has rectangles of color, each framed with a yellow line, the colors moving across the rug in diagonals. Between are dark strips decorated with segmented octagons.

With a leap of imagination, and encouraged by the late-twentieth-century explosion of bright color in all elements of interior decoration, people buying rugs have recognized that gabbehs have an incomparable quality of their own. Kilims, too, are at home in a modern setting. But unlike modern kilims, whose appearance is closely related to the patterns created over previous decades and centuries, gabbehs are uncompromisingly contemporary, while having a place in a magnificent tradition. The gabbeh has a long, luxurious pile, and this too has endeared it to a generation of householders who are enthusiastic for wooden, tiled, and other bare floors, but not averse to a touch of sensory pampering here and there.

Some gabbehs have a border, but this is often plain, undecorated color. Some have a design that continues to all the edges of the rug without a border to contain it. Some have a scattering of charmingly naive representations of animals and people, some have none and are entirely abstract. Abrashes (color changes caused by hand-spun dyed wool) are often particularly marked, as if the weaver has taken special pleasure in the variety of which the yarn is capable.

Among the most endearing and desirable patterns are those that describe an entire scene, which may be realistic or may be imagined. One such is the soccer match, with white lines depicting goalposts and boundary lines, two teams of figures in team colors, and a ball whose importance is signified by its (relatively) huge size. The fact that there are twelve figures on one team and ten on the other only serves to enhance the delight that the rug's design and coloring convey.

Not all new gabbehs have the quality of color and design demonstrated by the best, most vibrant examples woven in Iran. Some shops in the West offer for sale gabbehs that have been commissioned in colors that are a poor attempt at emulating the rich reds and creams of traditional tribal rugs. This is a misunderstanding of what the gabbeh is, and in visual

LEFT A small, traditional gabbeh charmingly eccentric in its design; the zig-zags on one side of the medallion are sharp and peaky, while on the other side they are sloping and languid.

BELOW A new gabbeh depicting the scene of a soccer match; the fact that there are twelve men in one team and only ten in the other does not detract from the rug's appeal.

terms it is a sad mismatch. These gabbehs are instantly recognizable for being drab and gloomy, conveying none of the life and brightness of their superiors. It is not even certain that they have been made in Iran. Whatever the case, they should be avoided.

Besides the emergence of new gabbehs, there is another, older, example of the influence that the demands of the Western market for Persian rugs has had upon the design of the rugs themselves. This is the Ziegler pattern, named after the Manchester-based English firm of Ziegler & Co., which opened offices in Arak (then known as Sultanabad) in north-central Iran in 1883.

Ziegler & Co. supplied weavers in that town with designs based on Persian decorative elements, adapted to the current taste in England for elegant, sinuous decoration incorporating leaves and flowers. This was apparent, too, in the work of the influential author and designer, William Morris. Like so much of the English public of that time, Morris was interested in Persian decoration and owned a famous rug that now hangs in the V&A Museum alongside the Ardebil Carpet.

Zieglers (the term continues to be used today, in Persian as well as in English) have a distinctive, open pattern of large and small fronds, arabesques, and repeating floral patterns.

Using a patterned rug in a decorating plan is easy, so long as the other colors in the room are compatible with the overall tone of the rug or kilim. If this is so, the rug should sit happily in its context. It need not be the only patterned item in the room, but it will look better on a floor of plain color.

KILIMS

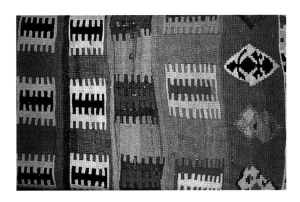

Opposite Kilims can be used not only on the floor but to furnish sofas and stools.

IN DECORATING TERMS, kilims are even more versatile than tribal rugs, because they are so supple. You can drape them over furniture and tables and, because they are lighter than pile rugs, they can easily be hung on the wall or used to cover doorways, in place of doors. They can be moved around the house, or carried into the garden, and they are usually less expensive than Persian pile rugs.

In theory kilims are not as hardwearing, because the pile on a rug protects its underlying structure, but, if treated with care, they will last as long as you want them to. They belong to a tradition that is even longer than that of pile rugs, and they should not therefore be seen as these rugs' poor relations. On the contrary, kilims offer a different but equally distinguished outlet for the talented weavers of the nomadic tribes of Iran, and other weavers.

A kilim is a flatweave, which is to say it has no pile but is simply a piece of flat woven textile. It is not, in other words, a knotted rug. Unlike a pile rug, where the supporting structure consists of the warp and weft, while the pile supplies the design on its surface, on a kilim structure and design are one. The weft is the pattern on almost all kilims.

Another type of flatweave, which the nomads of Iran make for themselves, is the jajim, a woven woolen cloth like a thick tablecloth or a thin picnic rug. These are usually made in strips, which are then sewn together to create a

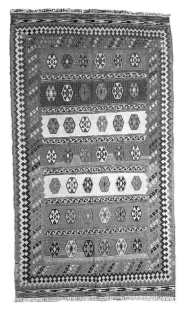

Above Blue is rarely used in old Kashgai kilims – this one is an exception.

85

LEFT Kilims are thinner and more supple than most rugs and drape well over a table. This kilim protects an antique table for everyday use.

OPPOSITE An exotic day bed is furnished with cushions formed from scraps of kilim.

larger piece. Jajims are used in much the same way as kilims, as wrapping for possessions, to cover nighttime gear during the day, and as room dividers. They are more loosely woven than kilims, and the designs are simple stripes (sometimes with a small repeated motif in a wide stripe) or plaids.

The loom is set up in exactly the same way for weaving a kilim as for a pile rug – horizontally on the ground if the weaver is a nomadic tribeswoman, vertically if she is a villager or possibly a settled nomad. The warp threads are attached to the loom and weaving begins. The wool used to weave kilims is generally of good quality, finely spun. As with rugs, mountain goats give the strongest, lustrous wool because they are spare, fit creatures.

The first inch or two may be woven using undyed wool that is not part of the design but, like the kilim on a pile rug, is intended to secure the weaving that follows. Then the color begins. Weft threads are woven in and out and beaten back in

the same way as the weft on a rug, except that they do not always go the whole way across the rug. Where the design dictates that the color changes, the weft thread is turned back on itself and woven back in the direction from which it came, and so on.

Thus areas of color are built up in blocks, rather than level across the whole piece. This contrasts sharply with a pile rug, which is, of practical necessity, worked up the rug in complete rows of knots. On a kilim, where the vertical side of one shape in the design ends and another (or the background color) begins, there is a tiny gap, right through from the back of the rug to the front, because there is no yarn joining one color to the next. When each block of color is finished, the end of the yarn is neatly turned in, so that there are no loose ends and the rug looks virtually the same on the back as it does on the front.

This results in a kilim having small narrow slits all across the pattern, which are apparent if you hold the kilim up to the

ABOVE Kilims with Kashgai designs, such as the two on these pages, are woven not only by the tribeswomen themselves, on the hillsides and in villages, but by others in south-western Iran such as the Lori and Afshar tribes.

light. This technique of weaving kilims is therefore known as "slitweave." On a well-designed piece this does not weaken the structure because the shapes are not large, and every diagonal or horizontal line immediately introduces weft threads that will once again link the two parts.

If the design involves lines along its length, the edge of a border for example, a line is made using one of the other techniques described below, or the weaver simply crenellates it. This means she moves the dividing line between the two colors, by two weft threads to the right and then, every quarter inch or so (or more if she wants), back to the left again. On close inspection the result looks like tiny castle battlements running up the rug. The practical effect is to secure the rug so that it only has short slits, which helps to keep the structure rigid.

The other techniques used to change from one color to another on a kilim include interlocking or dovetailing, where the two colors share a common warp thread, and double-interlocking, where they do not share a warp thread but they loop around each other before returning to their own block of color. Instead of the kilim having slits in it, both these techniques result in very small ridges on the rug because there is a double thickness of yarn where the threads interlock. These methods are more unusual – most kilims available in the West are slitweaves – and none dramatically alters the appearance of the rug, or how you should treat it.

Pattern on a kilim is generally geometric because of the technical limitations, but this does not seem to constrain the

RIGHT An exceptionally attractive Kashgai kilim, woven by a woman with a rare eye for design. She has used plenty of orange as well as the traditional red. The border and the lozenges formed from triangles contribute to the well-balanced overall effect. Weavers in northwest Iran are well known for using triangles in this way, but not the Kashgai.

weavers. Instead, their imaginations produce wonderfully varied designs, often consisting of a single or similar geometric motif repeated across the field of the rug, allowing repetition and color to make a powerful impact. Shapes and figures that often appear include diamonds, triangles, lozenges, crenellations, comb shapes, stars, birds, hooks or "running dog" motifs, the tree of life or, occasionally, a particularly interesting kilim has rows of animals.

The color of kilims varies hugely, from the breathtakingly vibrant (these kilims rarely reach Western markets), to the dark and somber, with many bright and pale shades in between. Occasionally there is a splash of white in the design, which may have been introduced with cotton yarn, cotton being a brighter white than wool, which is really never less than cream.

New kilims often have soft, subtle blues and pinks, because this is believed to be what the Western market wants. Older kilims and those made by weavers for their own use have stronger colors, though these have sometimes faded. "Faded" color may be the result of years in the sun, or of chemical treatment to make them look old. It is very difficult to tell if this is the case, other than by using your eyes and looking at many kilims, until you can see the differences, and then you can decide for yourself which you prefer.

As with pile rugs, certain tribes make certain styles of kilim, though divisions of style have broken down over generations with the movement of people and ideas, and some motifs are universal. Among the finest kilims are those made by the

RIGHT A splendid old Persian kilim with a wide band of decorative brocading at each end next to the fringe, and unusual knots, like tufts, on some of the central squares. The design is interesting: the pattern is not repeated evenly along the length of the kilim and the squares around each intruding point of the border are whittled away to make room.

DECORATING WITH

OPPOSITE AND RIGHT
A Kurdish kilim from
north western Iran
(right) and a detail of a
recent Kashgai creation
(opposite). Kurdish

kilims such as this are
tough and hardwearing,
because of the quality
of the wool, and they
last and wear
exceptionally well.

Afshar tribe, the Shahsavan (typically banded with stripes across, some containing whole or part stars), the Kashgai (old kilims are bold, pink and red – also sometimes orange – with hexagons containing stylized scorpions; new ones have plenty of blue), and the Lori (bold overall pattern, like their rugs, with complex borders).

The Balouch tribe makes rugs that often have a small strip of kilim up each side, woven from goats' hair; the story is that this protects you from snakes, as the goats' hair irritates them so they come no further than the edge. In the past, Kurdi Gouchan rugs were sometimes made with a broad strip of kilim up each edge, leaving a rectangular island of pile standing up in the middle (this is rarely seen on modern rugs).

The town of Senneh is well known for the quality of its kilims (with a typical pattern of a central medallion and all-over flower design), as is Veramin (cotton warp and weft, dark greens, blues, and brown, tending to be long and narrow). None of these elements is unique to any one tribe – it is the combination of all aspects of the design that indicates who might have made a kilim or rug.

Most kilims are weft-faced. This means that there are many more weft than warp threads per inch across the rug, so that the weft threads cover the warp threads and provide the color and pattern. Some kilims, however, are warp-faced. This means that there are more warp than weft threads, and it is thus the warp threads (running the length of the rug) that we see on the surface of the rug. A balanced weave is one in which there are equal numbers of warp and weft threads, and both

LEFT This splendid kilim is unusual because it is decorated with crosses, which look embroidered, and also because it is warp-faced. This means that there are more warp than weft threads per inch, so that the color is provided primarily by the warp. To illustrate this further, the abrashes (streaky color changes) lie along the warp instead of side to side.

are usually dyed. This produces a speckled surface if they are different colors. If warp and weft are the same color and the wool is hand-spun, this results in a single color surface of great depth and beauty.

When there are abrashes (color changes caused by hand-spun dyed wool — see page 64) on a warp-faced or balanced-weave kilim, these offer an unusual point of interest. Abrashes usually run from side to side on a rug. In this case, however, they run the length of the rug, because it is the warp threads that give the kilim its overall color. Decoration on a warp-faced or balanced-weave kilim is likely to be some form of brocading.

Some kilims, and the kilim sections on some pile rugs, are decorated with borders and motifs executed in what looks at a glance like embroidery. This is known as brocading (the Iranian word for this refers to "necklace," because the brocading looks not unlike a jeweler's filigree work). It is not added onto the kilim afterwards, as might appear, but is made as part of the weaving process. Colored weft threads are introduced into a particular place, often leapfrogging several warp threads to create part of a pattern. These are in addition to the regular weft threads that provide the kilim's structure. Sirjan kilims from southeastern Iran are often brocaded.

Other types of decoration on kilims involve various complicated forms of weft wrapping, where supplementary weft threads are wound around other threads to add motifs or lines of definition to a design. These include compound weft wrapping (two or more threads wrapping together), alternating

BELOW The "gabbim," an
unusual hybrid between
a gabbeh (the borders,
the animals, and the
tree of life) and a kilim
(the pinkish field has no
pile).

weft wrapping (around two threads, back up between them
and over two more, and so on), and many others which,
realistically, are too obscure (though often beautiful) to
concern anyone other than the expert. If you find a kilim you
like that has been made using an unusual technique, however,
do examine the front and back carefully and question the
dealer about it. Discover for yourself the intricacies of kilim
construction. Kilim sizes have the same names as rug sizes (see
page 49), though in reality there is less variation in kilim than
pile rug sizes.

It is not unknown for a weaver to experiment, creating, for
example, a curious and attractive hybrid between a kilim and a
gabbeh. This we could perhaps playfully call a "gabbim." One
such example has gabbeh-type borders and one-color kilim
field. On the field appear five figures – four sheep or lambs
(two near the top, two near the bottom) and in the middle a
tree of life. This last motif rarely appears either on new
gabbehs or on kilims. These five figures are all depicted in pile.

A rug such as this might be better suited to hanging on the
wall than lying on the floor, as the bulk of the borders and
figures might trip up the unsuspecting. It could also perhaps
be appreciated better hanging up, as it is a unique and
extraordinary piece.

The most dramatically different technique for weaving a
kilim is soumak. This is an intricate method of weaving that
involves using (usually) very fine weft threads and wrapping
them around warps and other wefts to create fine, delicate
designs that often look like embroidery or tapestries. A

DECORATING WITH

RIGHT Another fine, old kilim. Kilims were made to be used until they wore out, so old ones of good quality are special. This one has handsome brocading at each end, and knotted or plaited fringes. The crosses in the field are unusual and have no religious significance. The green background, too, is unusual – perhaps this piece was woven for a special occasion.

soumak kilim is instantly recognizable if you look at the back. The ends of wefts are not turned back in, as on a slitweave, but left dangling. The back of the kilim is a mass of loose threads. These should never be trimmed, as they are part of the rug as it was made by the craftswoman.

The fringes of kilims (as of rugs) can be plain, or they can be finished in a decorative fashion that can add considerably to their character and charm. Fringes are simply knotted, or netted (where knots are made from four wefts, for example, then divided into two, each pair being knotted with two from the neighboring knot, and so on). Plaited fringes are sometimes seen, some with the end of each plait bound in a contrasting color for extra decoration and visual impact. Occasionally a fringe is formed at one end of a kilim with loops of warp.

The floor is the first place where one thinks of placing a kilim. Unlike a pile rug, the color of the surface of the kilim will not be altered by the direction from which the light falls, so the tones will be the same whichever way you lay it. Because kilims are supple and relatively lightweight, however, they can be slippery on the floor, especially if it is polished wood. Tacky underlay helps, and if you find that a particular corner or edge tends to ride up, you can use double-sided carpet tape to secure this point (effectively to stick it down). There is nothing "wrong" with a kilim (or indeed a rug) that doesn't lie completely flat – its wrinkles are part of its character, and a reminder that it has been made by a human being, not a machine.

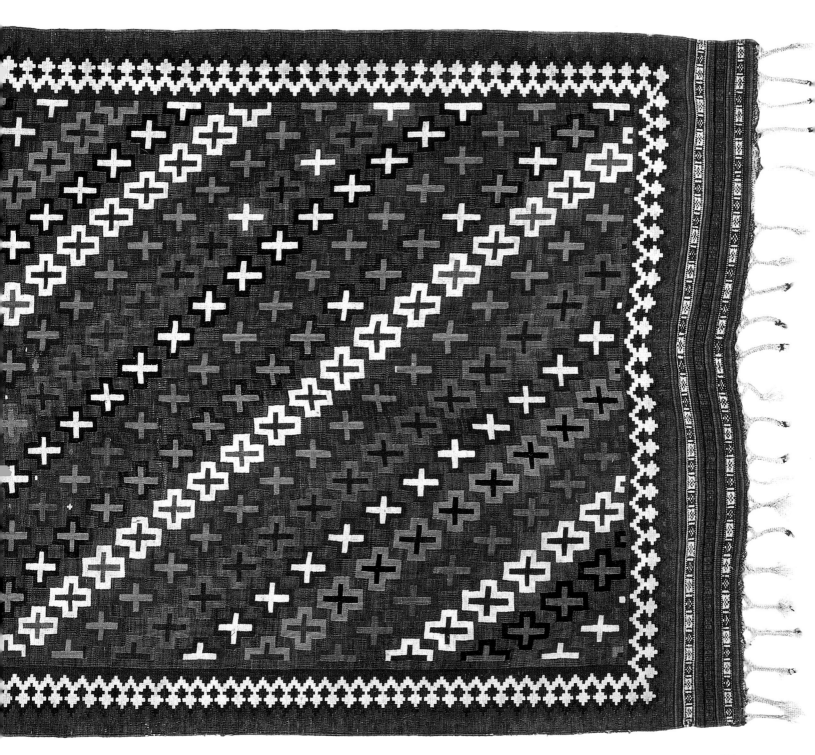

RIGHT An alcove at one end of this room has been made into a day bed with a kilim-covered base, bolsters, and cushions.

Provided the furniture has no sharp edges or rough corners that could damage the kilim, it can be placed straight on a table or chair without anything in between. If you are going to sit on it, however, an extra layer of, say, blanket or picnic rug will cushion the kilim and make it more comfortable. If the kilim is covering a table at which you eat, you could protect it at meal times by covering it with a cloth of compatible color and design, or with a tablecloth made of clear plastic. The latter will enable you to enjoy the kilim when sitting at table as well as protecting the kilim more effectively from spills.

One of the most lasting uses to which kilims, and indeed jajims, can be put is as upholstery fabric on sofas, chairs, and stools of all sorts. Their tight structure and the toughness of the wool of mountain sheep make them relatively indestructible as upholstery fabric. Lifted off the floor, to eye level if you are sitting down, the beauty of the color and design and the luster of the wool will be even more apparent. A

famous suite of furniture in Petworth House in England (a palatial seventeenth-century stately home now owned by The National Trust) is upholstered in kilim, laid over blue Utrecht velvet. The upholstery predates the 1950s and is in magnificent condition, as you would expect.

If you find a kilim that is damaged beyond repair in parts, the other parts may well be worth saving for a project such as upholstering a piece of furniture. If there is not enough to cover a whole chair, back and front, the back or outsides of the arms can be upholstered in another material, one whose color ties in well with the tone of the kilim.

Jajims of the type woven with stripes also make handsome upholstery. Check that the strips are sewn together securely and if necessary add a few stitches to secure them. The stripes and the substance and luster of the wool are reminiscent of eighteenth-century textiles, especially horsehair, and look as splendid on antique furniture as on modern.

Kilims and jajims can be used as curtains, in which case a strip of some other, fairly substantial fabric should be sewn across the back to give support, to which curtain rings should be attached. A preferable alternative is to sew a long pocket along the back and insert a rod through this, which is hinged where it is attached to the wall at one end. To open the curtain, you thus swing it rather than pulling it to one side.

In the course both of their daily life and of their biannual migration, nomadic tribespeople have a great need for bags. Bags (and to some extent small boxes) replace all the pieces of furniture in which house dwellers store their possessions: cupboards, chests of drawers, chests, shelves, and so on. Instead, nomads keep their belongings in bags of every size and shape, from ones small enough to fit in your pocket (for money or tobacco, perhaps) to capacious luggage in which to store your entire wardrobe. In between come bags for salt, precious possessions, jewelry, and all other belongings.

Then there are bags for the animals and migration – long narrow bags in which to transport the tent poles, bags containing food for the mules, donkeys, and (if you are a wealthy nomad) camels. All these bags are woven, some in kilim, some with pile or areas of pile, for example where the bag will rub against the sides of the mule. When a new bag is available (which can be before the old one has worn out), the old one is sold. Rug dealers occasionally have bags for sale. Alternatively, if you buy the smallest size of rug or kilim, or find a damaged kilim, you could have a bag made up specially out of the piece.

Straps of various sorts, woven in kilim, are also occasionally for sale. This type of strong, narrow "rope" is called tablet weaving and is made for such tasks as tying loads onto beasts of burden at migration. Sometimes a piece of tablet weaving has a large hand-carved wooden buckle-type structure at one end for securing the strap.

FLOORS

ABOVE An old-type gabbeh with an endearing pattern of medallions, placed more closely and regularly at one end of the rug than at the other, as if the weaver suddenly wanted to accelerate the speed of weaving.

THE FLOOR IS THE MOST OBVIOUS PLACE to put a rug – and the place for which it was intended, certainly if it is a pile rug. The wearing quality of a Persian tribal rug is not just good, it is excellent, partly because the piece will have been well crafted, but also because of the quality of the wool. As it gets older and is walked on and becomes worn, the crusty exterior of the fibers is worn away and the wool becomes shinier.

This luster is known as the "patina" and comes with age. Antique furniture has it too, and makers of reproduction furniture go to great lengths to try to reproduce it. Nothing, however, looks quite the same as a fine piece of craftsmanship that has mellowed naturally over many years.

There are two usual routes to placing a rug in your home. Either you have a room for which you want a rug, and you will search for a rug that suits; or you have a rug for which you want a room. This could be because you are moving to a new house, or because you have been bequeathed or given a rug, or because you have seen a rug with which you have fallen in love.

In the first case (finding a rug for a room), you are likely to need time to bring the look of the rug and the look of the room together. You would be very lucky to throw down the first rug you try and say "Perfect!" Any reputable rug dealer or shop will either let you borrow a rug or kilim on

OPPOSITE Rugs and kilims add a softening touch to this handsome and cavernous bedroom.

ABOVE The striped fringe here comes from the colored warp threads.

101

OPPOSITE The pattern of
this kilim, with its
indented zig-zags,
echoes the patterns
that the stairs make as
they rise up the wall.
This kilim will be seen
whole by anyone
coming down the stairs.

RIGHT Rugs laid on top of
each other or
overlapping create an
interesting patchwork
and also provide greater
insulation.

approval, to take it home and try it, or, more likely, sell it to you "on approval."

Buying a rug on approval means that you can return it and have a full refund, within a certain time limit – vital if you are to have the chance of laying the rug in your room for a while. This is really the only way of testing whether you like it and whether it is right for the room. There is no need to feel apologetic about trying several rugs in this way until you are satisfied with one, provided that you are serious about buying one of the rugs in the end.

The two aspects of a rug that make the greatest visual impact are its pattern and color. If you are buying from an honest and experienced dealer, your choice of pattern will be entirely a matter of taste, because she will have ensured that any rug she offers you is good quality within your price range. Color, however, is a different matter, and one that will draw on your own personal taste in such things. A rug or kilim

supplies a large block of colors, usually with one color or tonal range predominant. Consider the color carefully.

When you try a pile rug, remember that the color tones vary hugely depending on which way around the rug lies on the floor. This is because the pile of a rug does not stand exactly upright. When a rug is woven, a weft thread is inserted across each row of knots that form the pile, and is then beaten down with a heavy metal comb. Combined with gravity, this results in the pile pointing slightly down the rug to the edge where it was started. This end used to be known as the "front" of the rug and the end where it was finished the "back," but these terms are now old-fashioned and rarely used.

When you look at a rug from the end where it was started, towards which the pile lies, it looks darker because you are looking at the cut-off ends of the woolen fibers. When you look at the same rug from the other end, it looks lighter, because you are looking at the glossy, light-reflecting sides of

the tufts of wool. This can matter less if the rug has a design that looks as good from both ends. Kilims, too, more often than not have a design that makes sense equally well either way round as their motifs are generally geometrical or highly abstracted.

Some rugs, however, have a design of birds or other figures or motifs that makes better visual sense when you look at it from the end where the rug was begun. This is how the weaver saw it when she made it, after all. If the rug you are trying is "read" better from one end than the other, this will influence how you lay it and thus how you see the color.

Color also looks different according to the quality of the light. When you borrow a rug (or buy it on approval), have a look at it both in daylight and after dark, by electric light, in all the rooms where it might go. Walk all around it in both types of light so that you can see all its possible appearances. You will almost certainly find that both look completely different from their appearance in the shop or warehouse.

Another aspect of any rug is its size. It can be a useful experiment to try two rugs, one the size you thought you wanted, and one larger. A smaller rug may fit neatly into the space between your sofa and fireplace (for instance), but a larger one may unify the room better, bringing together all the smaller elements rather than adding another. If the rug or kilim is intended for a dining room or the eating area of a living room, it should be large enough for people to sit at the table and not catch the edge with their chairs. A dining area therefore usually needs a substantially sized rug or kilim.

A large rug may look more generous, by comparison with the smaller one that you thought you preferred. It can make a small room look large if it reaches to the walls rather than sitting in the middle, because it leads the eye to its edges. On the other hand, you don't want a rug that will overwhelm a room, and you may find your original opinion about size is confirmed and reinforced by experimenting with sizes.

Some rugs are not an exactly regular shape. A rug might be wider at one end than the other, or it might have an edge that is not straight. A kilim might have patches that wrinkle so that the surface is not flat on the floor. This is not a fault with the rug but rather adds to its attraction, showing that it is an individual, handmade piece, not something made in a factory. It may also mean that the rug was exported from Iran some decades ago, since stretching to regularize the shape is now a normal part of the finishing process in Iran for rugs destined for export to the West.

Today, a rug that is not regular in shape is dampened, then nailed to two boards side by side with one of them lifted slightly off the ground. When this board is dropped, the two pieces of wood sit together so tightly that the irregular part of the rug is stretched to conform with the rest. The reason for doing this is to satisfy the demand from customers for rugs that are, in some respects at least, as perfect as possible. In some ways this is a shame, as much of the charm of a rug lies in its individuality, flaws and all.

Ways can usually be found of laying a rug so that its imperfections are disguised, if this is what you want. Lay the

DECORATING WITH

OPPOSITE AND RIGHT Two magnificent rugs, the near one from Isphahan, the far one a Kashgai piece of rarely-seen design, without medallions or spandrels, its field crammed with creatures and vegetation.

RIGHT This old Persian or Caucasian rug lies well on a short-pile carpet, without wrinkling or curling at the edges.

straight edge of the rug where it is better seen than the crooked, or near the wall where the wall's straightness will not reproach the rug's irregularity. A bumpy patch of kilim can be hidden by a chair or table, rather than being placed near a doorway where it will wait to trip someone up.

Rugs can also be used to help resolve problem spaces and to define different spaces for different activities within one room. If you have an "L-shaped" room, for example, decide to which branch of the "L" the corner area belongs. Then lay a long rug that runs from the corner into that branch of the "L," unifying them. Place a smaller rug in the other branch to reinforce the visual message.

If you have a large family room or kitchen with areas for separate activities — sitting and eating, for example — these can be defined using rugs. A sitting area is the obvious place for a rug's or kilim's warmth and texture. Choose one that is large enough to embrace the entire seating area and this will mark

out a part of the room that is different. Alternatively, place your table and chairs on a rug (only if your children, if any, are old enough not to drop food at every meal), or corral your office desk and equipment here, to define this area.

Furniture can sit on a rug quite happily, providing you take various precautions to prevent the rug being damaged (see Chapter Ten: Laying, Care, and Repair, on page 140, for more information). It can even help keep the kilim in place and prevent it riding on a slippery floor. Very small rugs should be positioned with special care because they are easier to trip over, especially on a smooth floor such as polished wood, having more edges per square foot than large ones.

Certain places call for specific types of rug: hallways and passages for runners, for example. A runner is (as its name suggests) a rug that is long and narrow, conventionally at least two-and-a-half times as long as its width. Certain areas of Iran are known for making the most beautiful runners; the

Opposite The subdued browns and pinks of this runner go well with the other furnishings; in fact these colors are not popular with tribal weavers, and some of the browns may once have been blue that has faded with time.

Right The cushions on the sofa are made from Kashgai bag facings; the rug on the floor is a Persian gabbeh.

Hamadan district for example, and also various villages in northwest Iran such as Karaja, Lambaran, and Sarab.

The floor immediately in front of an open fire is another traditional home for a particular sort of rug – the hearthrug. This does not exist as a definition of a rug type; rather it is a Western idea to which Persian rugs have been made to conform. Any rug of suitable size will do, but an exceptionally valuable one is not usually placed here because of the danger of it being burned by sparks from the fire.

If you care about your rug and have taken trouble to choose it, the idea of it being damaged in this way will be alarming. Always use a fire screen fit for the job (not one that is too small or has holes in it), and remember that seasoned wool does not burn easily. If you remove the offending ember right away, or stamp out the spark, there should be little or no damage. A black spot is often the remains of the burnt matter, not singed wool, and can be scraped off or vacuumed away.

When you are satisfied with the rug's color, pattern, regularity, and size, it is time to lay it and live with it. This could also be an opportunity for you to rethink details of the room's decoration. Remove all but large items of furniture and return the pieces carefully, being sure that you want them back in the room, and that they are in the right place. A new element like a rug or kilim can act as a catalyst, creating an atmosphere that welcomes change.

If, on the other hand, you are moving or have fallen in love with a rug, you may have to do a certain amount of redecorating in sympathy with the tones of your floorcovering. When you get it home, put the rug or kilim in place and consider its color context. Walls that you thought were cream can suddenly look too white for the rug, or red walls too yellow or too blue. Whatever you decide to do, don't rush into it. The rug or kilim may have been waiting decades to arrive in this room; take your time deciding how to accommodate it.

LEFT In general, the bathroom is not a good place to keep a rug, as prolonged exposure to dampness will damage it, but this rug is small and can easily be taken out to air and ensure it is thoroughly dry.

OPPOSITE The kilim on the floor of this exotic bedroom has an unusual feature – the pattern on the separate stripes of color looks as if it has been embroidered afterwards; in fact it is created as part of the weaving process by the technique known as weft wrapping.

You may be surprised, however, to find that the rug or kilim fits well into your existing room design, especially if you have a distinctive taste in color or style. Both the appearance of your home, and your choice of a rug in this particular style and color, will have been informed by your taste. Tastes change, however, and develop with age and experience. A collection of rugs and kilims built up over the years will reflect this and carry with it the story of your life during that time.

Of course, any choice of rug is not final. You can sell or otherwise dispose of a rug, though you probably will not want to if you have loved it. Move your rugs around from room to room after a few years. You will see them all in a new light. Alternatively, fulfill the rug-lover's dream: have rugs and kilims in reserve so that you can change them with the seasons. Rich, warm colors in winter can give way to bright reds and greens or subtle pinks and blues in summer. Change the rugs on your floors according to your mood.

WALLS
AND
ELSEWHERE

OPPOSITE This room is made exotic and colorful by the addition of a collection of rugs and kilims from the region, which also pull the room together visually – rugs on the floor and kilims on the sofas.

THERE ARE VARIOUS WAYS of hanging rugs and kilims on walls, and many other uses to which you can put them besides simply laying them on the floor. Kilims in particular are made by Iran's nomadic tribes for a range of uses such as covering bedding and other possessions during the day, sleeping under during the night, and dividing areas within the tent, but not for laying on the ground. For this they make and use pile rugs.

Kilims are also lighter than pile rugs, which makes them easier to handle and move, and marginally better suited to being hung up for any great length of time because less strain is put upon them. The tight construction of most tribal pile rugs, however, means that absolutely no harm is done to them by hanging on the wall, provided it is done carefully. Hanging up a rug or kilim undoubtedly looks dramatic and gives you the chance to appreciate its whole design, uninterrupted by people and furniture, and enjoy it as a work of art.

There are several methods used to hang rugs and kilims on the walls, and you may be able to invent yet more. The simplest depends upon that prosaic item required for laying fitted carpet – the gripper strip. This is a strip of wood with nails sticking out of it, designed to be laid around the perimeter of a room, where it grips the edges of the flooring. Cut a piece that is just slightly shorter than the width or length of your rug or kilim (depending on

ABOVE A new gabbeh with human and animal figures. The triangular structure near the center may be a nomadic school tent, a circular, open-sided tent.

117

LEFT A kilim or rug can
be hung on a wall in
various ways; a gripper
rod designed to secure
carpet around the
edges of a room is
invisible and possibly
the easiest to install.

OPPOSITE The handsome
kilim on the main wall of
this room is as
interesting as any
picture, and links visually
with the rest of the
room through the kilims
on floor and ottoman.

which way you want to hang it) and screw it to the wall. Use plugs appropriate to the material from which the wall is built, as well as to the weight of the rug. Lift your rug, press the appropriate edge against the length of the gripper strip, and gently let go.

A more traditional method and one that gives equally good support is to sew a strip of tough fabric onto the back of the rug, along the edge from which you want to suspend it, leaving the ends open. Sewing something onto the rug will not damage it. You can then run a strong pole such as a brass rail or copper plumbing pipe through this "pocket" and attach the ends to the wall or the ceiling. Alternatively, cut vertical slits at intervals along the fabric pocket, push a pole into the pocket, and hang it from hooks inserted through the slits.

Yet another option is to grip the rug with metal clamps and hang it from these. Some rug shops and warehouses use this method to display their goods. You can also sandwich the top of the rug between two narrow strips of wood and clamp these together.

One method that is not recommended is to sew curtain or other rings directly onto the back of the piece: they will eventually pull the rug or kilim out of shape and damage it. If you want to use rings, sew a strip of hardwearing, tightly woven fabric onto the back of the rug as before, then attach the rings to this. The simplest, most basic method of hanging a rug is to nail it straight on to the wall with tacks, though this cannot be recommended because it will eventually pull the rug out of shape.

OPPOSITE A long kilim makes a magnificent curtain, hung from a rod near the ceiling and draped back to one side during the day.

LEFT This grand drawing room shows how different patterns used cleverly can work together, creating an effect of luxury and sophistication. On the floor is a Persian piece. The wall hanging is probably an Indian embroidery on velvet, and the box table is covered with bits of old rug, also from Iran.

The next decision is where to hang it. This will easily be answered if you have chosen a rug specifically for a particular site in your home. More often than not, however, deciding to hang a rug is an afterthought to deciding to buy it. Space is usually the initial criterion. A rug that looks quite a normal size on the floor can seem to need a huge amount of wall space, as if it were a very large picture. This may mean you can only hang small rugs, but if you have a large space available, a rug or kilim can easily fill it. Hung over a focal point, such as a fireplace, or in a prominent position, a beautiful rug will have all the attention it deserves.

Rooms with high ceilings, or walls that rise through more than one floor of a building, are both obvious locations. Stairwells can offer sufficient space, but the problem with these is that you often cannot get far enough away from the piece to see its overall design properly, or even see the whole thing in one glance. Then there is the danger of it being curled or worn if it hangs so that you tend to catch a corner or rub against it going up and down the stairs.

One important consideration is that the wall you choose must be dry. Getting damp, without the opportunity of getting thoroughly dry again, is one of the main enemies of textiles in general, including kilims and rugs. This makes them unsuitable for steamy rooms such as bathrooms and kitchens. Kitchens are also considered inappropriate because of the likelihood of there being grease in the air, however tiny the amount.

Kilims (usually in preference to rugs, which are generally stiffer and less easy to pull to one side) can be hung over a doorway in place of a solid door. If you want it "open," fix a pole or loop on one side over which to drape the kilim. Alternatively, hang it by the fabric-strip-and-ring method on a pole, so that you can draw it completely to one side of the doorway like a curtain. The visual advantage that a kilim has

RIGHT Hang a kilim on the wall behind the head of a bed to give it a sense of drama and importance.

over a curtain, and indeed a pile rug, is that it looks the same on the back as it does on the front (unless it is a soumak kilim, with the ends of the different colored yarns hanging loose on the back).

Old houses often suffer from draftiness. Rugs and kilims can help solve this problem. An external door can be made more draft-proof by having a kilim hung across it, covering the edges. A remnant of kilim could also be used as extra draft-proofing by being sewn into a sausage shape and stuffed with a couple of small bricks (for weight) and some padding. Place this across the bottom of the offending door.

Other woven artifacts such as bags can also be hung on walls. A collection hung in an arrangement together always makes more impact than dotting them around a room or through the house. Another interesting woven item made by the nomads is a baby's cradle. This is a rectangular panel with loops across each end, through which rods are inserted, from

which the cradle is suspended and swung to rock the baby, who lies in the middle of the piece, on the back of the pile. A well-crafted cradle has many tassels hanging down from the ends and at intervals across the pile underneath. When the cradle is in use, the tassels swing and deter flies and animals from disturbing the child.

In a bedroom, kilims make handsome bed covers, and are warm to sleep under in winter. This is, after all, one of the main uses to which the nomads themselves put them, bringing them out and laying them on the rocks or grass to air in the morning, splashing the hillside around a nomad's tent with brilliant color.

A kilim or rug can also be hung on the wall at the head of a bed to impressive effect. This will give the bed an importance it did not have before, especially if it is a divan. Be careful, though, to supply plenty of pillows or cushions as a backrest when sitting up in bed; you don't want to pull down

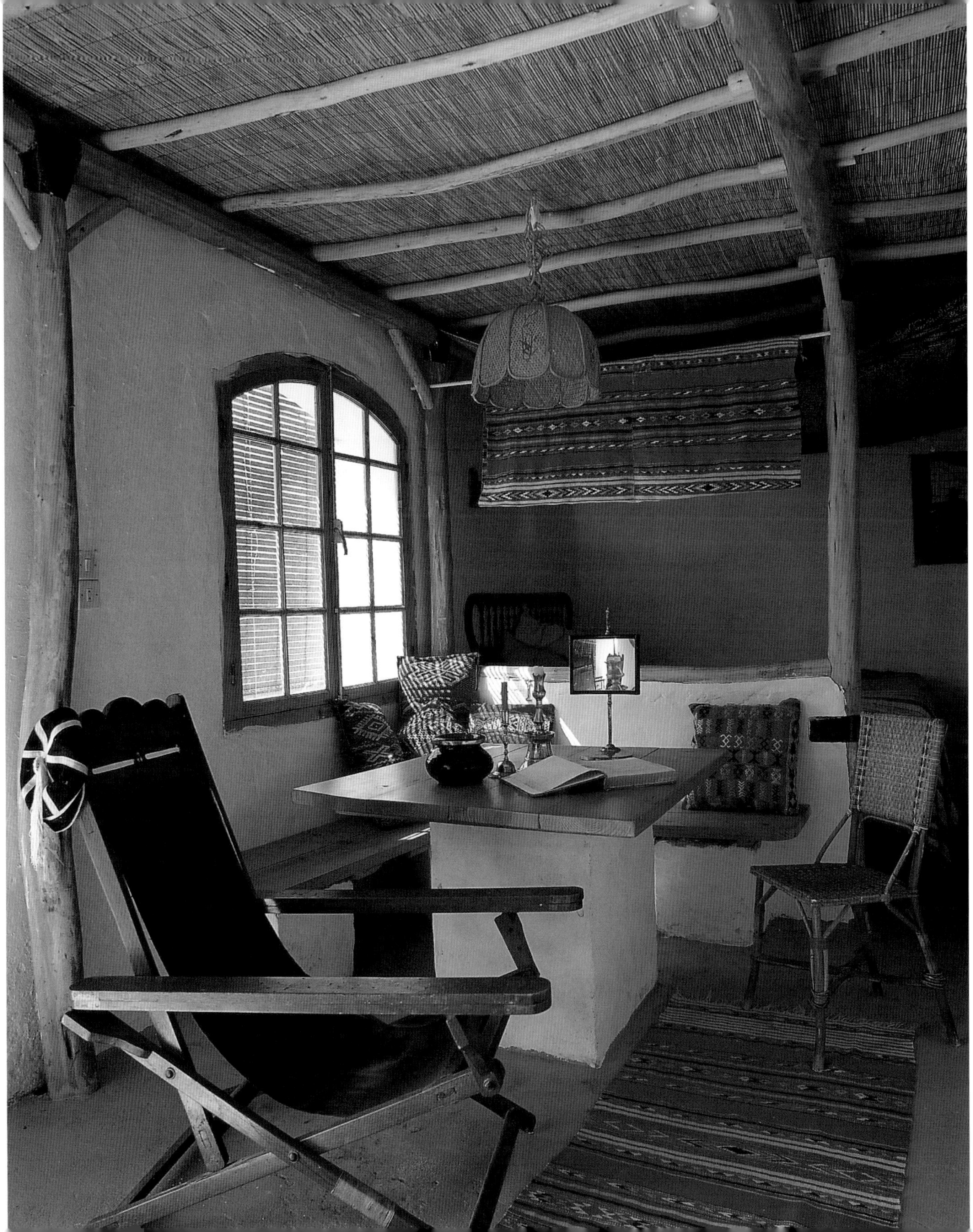

OPPOSITE The color and pattern of a handsome kilim thrown on a wide, plain sofa makes it the focus of a spacious, modern interior that is otherwise decorated in white and neutral tones.

LEFT The vegetable-dyed colors of the pieces of kilim used to make these cushions glow against the battered brown leather of an old sofa in an English country cottage.

on the rug and cause it stress in this way, and it is better if your head doesn't touch or rub against the rug. In a room where a divan doubles as a sofa, hang a rug lengthwise along the wall behind it to make it seem less bedlike during the day.

Kilims can, of course, be hung as curtains at a window. Before deciding to do this, experiment by hanging your kilim temporarily over the window, to discover how lightproof it really is. The wool parts may well be almost impenetrable, but if it is a slitweave, the small gaps may let in too much light for your taste. On the other hand, you may like the new design you see when the surface of the kilim is in darkness, but light gleams through the pattern of slits in the early morning.

A rug or kilim hung from the ceiling to the floor can help with storage space. Hang it across an awkward corner, a recess or space under the stairs, to create a "cupboard" behind, or use across the front of a fitted wardrobe. Position it slightly away from the wall and create a place for keeping tall, slim

household items like the ironing board, airing racks, folding chairs, or coats hanging on pegs. Or fix it in front of open shelves on which you can store less-than-beautiful but nonetheless necessary household items like light bulbs, cleaning materials (providing that none of these will touch the hanging), and sewing things.

An alternative to attaching a rug rigidly to the wall or ceiling, and to hanging it on rings so it will gather like a curtain, is to hang it from a runner. This way, the top can remain flat, yet you can draw the curtain to one side for access to storage space behind.

Hanging a kilim up across part of a room can help unify a large room that is actually used for several different purposes – a living room that is also a playroom, or a spare bedroom that doubles as an office. The playroom elements, such as plastic crates of toys and paints, can be stored on shelves and the rug hung either from the ceiling or from the top of the

125

LEFT An old Caucasian piece, worn bare in patches and with a raggedy broken selvage, has found a new lease on life as a tablecloth or protector.

OPPOSITE The kilim on the table is interesting in that it appears to have been cut in two and reattached. In fact it was made in two pieces, the loom not being wide enough to make it in one.

shelving unit. An office area can be disguised in a similar way, with a hanging rug or kilim hiding desk, paperwork, computer, filing system and all.

Alternatively, if you keep your desk immaculate, you could simply drape a kilim over an unsightly filing cabinet (or spray-paint it to join the room's color scheme). Don't drape a kilim over a computer, however; it is too heavy and not sufficiently dustproof. Minute loose fibers or dust trapped in the weaving could actually damage your system.

A kilim can of course be used to cover any table – or you can make a table to a specific size to display a kilim. A piece of board on a basic timber frame, or a cheap prefab chipboard table of the type intended to be covered up, will suffice perfectly, providing that the edges are smooth and not likely to wear or damage the rug. Watch out too for possible damage to the fringe. Ideally, this will brush the floor rather than draping on it, so that it doesn't get trodden on.

A kilim can be draped over any piece of furniture to hide or disguise it – or simply to provide a visual change. A brightly colored kilim thrown over a sofa upholstered in subdued colors will give you a change of scene to cheer up dull winter months or in keeping with bright summer sunshine. The toughness and resilience of kilim also make it ideal for upholstering chairs, sofas, and stools (more about this in Chapter Six: Kilims, on page 85). Small rugs or fragments of kilim can find a use as the fronts of cushions.

With a long kilim, you can create a magnificent four-poster bed, using a simple timber frame. The overhead part of the

OPPOSITE You can either cover a sofa completely with a large kilim or drape a kilim or throw over part of it, either for decoration or to disguise an area of wear and tear. Either way, the kilims, and indeed the cushions and rug on the floor, make this room warm and welcoming.

LEFT The kilim on the floor of this drawing room, with its trellis of linked flowers, is an unusual antique piece from Turkey, which will soon be a museum piece as kilims this old are increasingly rare.

frame probably needs to have bars or beams across it at generous intervals, to support the weight of the kilim and prevent it from drooping down in the middle. Hang the kilim down the head and foot of the frame and drape it along the bars, an equal amount between each.

If you are using a kilim or rug as a room divider, as the nomads do, choose one that will reach from floor to near the ceiling. As when covering a table, it is better if the kilim doesn't actually drape on the floor, as its fringe may be trodden on and damaged. Or, if you want to retain the illusion of space, hang a smaller kilim from a custom-made rod or frame, or attach it to a partition, so that it falls to the floor from a place below the height of the ceiling. Thus it will act as a screen, but your eye will see that there is more beyond, contributing to a feeling of spaciousness.

If you want to create an impression of being in a nomad's tent, you can always attach a kilim to the ceiling itself. Nomad's tents don't actually have ceilings made of kilim; the effect is only that – a decorating effect. Your ceiling should not be too high, where the kilim would look silly, or too low, where, if you are tall, you may brush your head against it. A ceiling of 10 feet would be ideal. Use a staple gun or tacks to attach it to the ceiling in as many places as possible, to spread the weight.

129

OUTDOORS

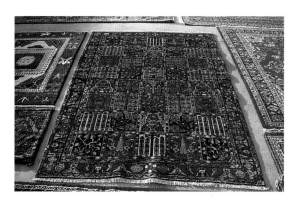

OPPOSITE Rugs make the floor of a tent warm and welcoming – whether it is a Kashgai nomad's tent or a Westerner's summer pavilion.

PERSIAN RUGS AND KILIMS have gained a certain image in the decades since they once again became such a rich and rewarding source of interest. It is easy to imagine a tribal rug in front of an open fire surrounded by upholstered armchairs and polished antique furniture. Now, however, homemakers and interior designers have discovered that kilims and gabbehs, especially, are equally at home in contemporary interiors and settings where their bright color makes a vital contribution.

The next place to take a kilim is outdoors. It may come as a surprise to realize that there is no reason why you should not take a rug or kilim out into the open air, or into an outdoor building, providing you use a degree of common sense in planning where to put it.

Persian tribal nomads, after all, take their kilims out of the tent in the morning to air them after sleeping under them, spreading them out on grass or bushes or rocks — whatever their surroundings consist of in the place where they have camped. And later, when the rugs they have sold to an agent have been treated in a washing factory, they are spread out on the ground to dry in the sun. Some are even spread on the roof of the factory if it is flat and accessible. Every square foot of space is made to work.

So, though our rugs are precious to us, they are not objects of such delicacy that they can only be brought out on special occasions, like a fine

ABOVE As part of the process of preparing rugs for export from Iran, they are laid in the sun to dry. Prolonged exposure to sunlight, even in a temperate climate, will cause them to fade, but occasional use outdoors should not cause them any damage. This is a fine Bakhtiar rug with a garden design.

LEFT A rug on the floor of a lavish summer house.

china tea set. To the nomads they are everyday furniture, as much used as our kitchen tables. As far as rugs are concerned, the vital difference between Iran and the temperate countries for which the nomads' weavings are so often destined is the climate.

Dampness is the enemy of the tribal rug or kilim – not the getting wet, so much as the being damp. As we have seen, the rugs are completely soaked through when they are washed, but afterwards they are thoroughly dried. So long as it is not wet for long, and properly dried afterwards, the rug comes to no harm. We wash our woolen sweaters regularly without damage. The danger to a rug or kilim comes when it is not allowed to dry all the way through; the result can be mold, rot, and mildew, or cracking and splitting later when the rug finally does dry out.

The obvious solution is not to allow the rug to get wet in the first place. Take your rugs out only on a day when the weather is fine, and if you are using them on the ground like picnic rugs, always lay down an impervious undersheet first. This could be wide plastic sheeting bought from a garden center, or it could be a tarp of the variety sold in camping shops. Any type of material is fine, so long as it is waterproof and does not have tears or holes in it.

Experiment with different types, if you can, to find one that does not make a crinkly noise when you walk or sit on the rug, and one that does not cause the rug or kilim to slip off it. Lay the sheet on the ground and the rug on top of it, folding back any bits of plastic that stick out from under the rug, so that they are just hidden. The plastic will also prevent the kilim or rug from picking up dust or sand from the ground.

If you have a kilim that you regularly use in this way and that is not especially valuable, and a plastic sheet that is not used for any other purpose, you could consider stapling the plastic to the rug, at intervals around the edges. Purists might

RIGHT This rug furnishes
the floor of an outside
courtyard.

LEFT This pool house has a beautiful, old Persian kilim in the entrance area, seen here glowing in the sun. In general, though, beware of sunshine damaging your rugs and kilims.

OPPOSITE The design of this old rug is in sympathy with the regular pattern of tiles both around the fountain and on the walls of this courtyard in a house in North Africa.

be horrified, but if it works for you and makes it easier to use the rug, why not? Check the staples regularly to ensure that they are not going rusty, as this would damage the kilim. Check the plastic for tears or holes. And, naturally, avoid using the rug in a position or on a day when it is likely to get damp, in spite of these other precautions.

If the plastic is stapled to the kilim, it cannot breathe or dry out on that side. In fine weather, condensation may appear, especially if the ground is cool and the air hot. Keep it in the shade, check for condensation, and remove the plastic sheeting during the winter months. If you use the type of little gadget designed to open staples before removing them, you should be able to do this with no damage to the rug and minimal damage to the plastic sheet.

Kilims are better suited to being outdoors than rugs for several reasons. They are lighter and more easily carried around; they are more supple and adapt easily to being draped over furniture and uneven ground; and they do not have a pile in which to gather dirt, grass seed, dust, sand, or any other particles carried by a breeze, lifted off the ground, or transported on the bare (or indeed shod) human foot.

Rugs can be used outdoors, especially very worn ones where hardly any pile remains. Unless such a rug is valuable for historical reasons or because it is particularly fine or beautiful, using it outdoors can give it an extra lease on life when it might otherwise be consigned to a dark attic or storeroom. Badly worn rugs can be picked up cheaply at local sales and auctions — to most people a rug without a pile seems useless

Kilims and woven cloths contribute to the air of relaxed exoticism in this outbuilding converted, for the summer, to an outdoor room for sleeping or lounging.

LEFT A Persian miniature dating from at least the sixteenth century shows pupils learning the Koran in a garden. The master, as befits his status, sits or kneels on a rug.

and almost worthless – quite possibly more cheaply than an ordinary run-of-the-mill picnic rug.

Kilims and rugs laid on the ground and over tables can turn a picnic into a party. They lend style and a degree of grandeur to an occasion. If you cover ordinary trestle or garden tables with kilims, they look fit for a banquet. Check that the table beneath is clean, dry, and does not have any sharp edges or loose splinters that could damage the kilim. If in doubt, cover the table with a plastic sheet or another cloth first.

Where food and drink are concerned, you will probably want to lay a tablecloth over the kilim to protect it from spillages, whether on a serving table or for a picnic on the ground. A clear, plastic cloth will allow the beauty of the rug to be seen through it; a cotton or linen cloth will complement the natural fibers of the rug.

Another temporary arrangement for a kilim or rug is to fling it over a garden bench or chair. Not only will it transform the look of the furniture, especially if it is plastic, but it will make it more comfortable to sit on by softening the edges. An ordinary bench dressed with a brightly colored kilim and some cushions becomes a throne fit for a king or queen, and certainly a place that invites you to put up your feet and relax with a good book or the Sunday newspaper.

Some outdoor locations beg, by their very nature, for a rug or kilim to create warmth and a sense of place. A summerhouse, enclosed loggia, or other outdoor building with a stone or wooden floor will become a place of warmth and color if you introduce a rug or kilim.

A rug laid in a greenhouse is likely to fade more than one in an indoor room. And in winter, when the windows and doors to the garden tend to be closed, condensation can cause a rug or kilim to become damp. So long as you are aware of these dangers, and find ways to circumvent them (blinds, for example, and good ventilation in winter), there is no reason why you cannot lay a rug or kilim in a greenhouse. If the floor is covered with terracotta tiles, or natural material such as stone or slate, the rug will look splendid.

A treehouse large enough to lay a rug in is many a child's (and adult's) dream. Providing that you can construct a system for getting the rug or kilim up there in the first place, and that you take the usual precautions against it becoming damp, there is no reason why your treehouse should not be thus furnished. Removing it in winter would be a sensible action. Animals and birds who move in when you or your children move out for the season will do serious damage, never mind the dampness.

And, finally, why should your use of a kilim or rug be confined to daytime activity? If the nomads who made them use their rugs to lie on in their tents at night, as they do, why shouldn't you? Likewise kilims: Iran's tribal nomads sleep under a cover that is something like a cross between a comforter and down quilt, with a kilim on top. On the chilliest night, under the stars in a clear sky, the kilim, which is denser than the best woolen blanket, will help to keep you warm, from your toes right up to your chin. Above there, you will have to think of another method of keeping yourself snug.

SECTION 3:

PRACTICALITIES

Opposite Kilims used in a variety of ways to furnish a patio – as upholstery on chairs and stools, as cushions, even as slippers.

Left The capital of Iran, Tehran, does not produce great quantities of rugs, which makes this piece, probably created in the early twentieth century, interesting. It is elaborate and detailed, and the color has a somber intensity.

LAYING, CARE, AND REPAIR

Hunting for the carpet that is precisely what you want, or deciding exactly how to make the most of a rug that you already have, is an exhausting business. You've got it home, and it looks great (so often rugs look even better at home than they do in the shop or warehouse). You are ready to relax and enjoy it. First, though, there are some practical matters to consider, matters pertaining to the long-term life of your rug or kilim.

The comparison has often been made between rugs and wine. Like fine wine, rugs can take some time to reach maturity, quietly developing and improving as the years go by. In the case of a rug, this is partly because the light friction caused to its surface by people walking on it is good for it. In effect, footsteps polish the wool, which gradually acquires a deep sheen known as the patina.

Once it has reached maturity, which might take twenty years after its creation, a rug should remain at its peak for at least another couple of decades, providing you look after it. Indeed, if you really care for it, paying it attention rather than taking it for granted, there is no reason why it should not give pleasure to future generations.

If the rug is in good condition, the first consideration is the floor itself, on which the kilim or rug will lie. If this is not entirely flat, or if after trying the rug in position you find that it wrinkles and rides up, you may need an underlay. In Iran people do not generally use underlay for their rugs, though the nomads often have layers of plastic and felt rugs under theirs, because they are laying them directly on the ground.

Pile rugs are less likely to need underlay than kilims, which are lighter, have less body, and are supple. All these qualities are advantages in some circumstances, such as when you use a kilim to drape over a sofa or table. On the floor, however, this means that they wrinkle and slip more easily than rugs, especially on polished floors. A kilim laid on a polished wooden floor where people walk can be positively dangerous, causing you to slip and fall. An underlay is vital here.

On hard floors such as stone, tiles, or slate, a kilim needs an underlay as a form of protection; without it the structure is squeezed against the hardness of the floor every time you walk on it. A kilim does not have a pile to protect it from this pounding.

A pile rug, on the other hand, is generally better off without certain sorts of underlay. If this is too deep, for example, the rug is flexed and dented every time it is walked on, which eventually causes it stress. Rubber and felt underlays can also be less than helpful – poor quality rubber can disintegrate after a few years, breaking off in little pills, and it can become sticky, which is anathema to wool rugs. The fibers of felt underlay can work themselves into the body of the rug, and also create dust. Pile rugs mostly don't need underlay – their pile and structure help keep them flat – unless they are delicate.

The most interesting underlays are the most modern. New types appear regularly, the best of which are lightweight and slim rather than heavy and bulky. Other types use new synthetic materials, which have sometimes been developed for quite another use. One, for example, is a wafer-thin material that feels like flexible matte plastic. When you fly in an airplane you may find a small sheet of this on your plastic food tray, designed to prevent the dishes (and your cup of coffee in particular) from sliding around.

Ask the person who sold you your rug for a personal recommendation; ask a dealer whom you think is up-to-date on these things; and consult anyone you know who has rugs in their home about what they use and how successful it is. You may have to do some research, as dealers' opinions vary, and new non-slip underlays are being developed all the time. There may well be a brand-new product available that is better than all the others.

Of all the surfaces that rugs can lie on, machine-made carpet is amongst the most trouble-free. The shorter the pile, the better for the rug. Persian tribal rugs look best on a completely plain floor of whatever type. They also look fine on natural floorings — that is to say, matting made of sisal, coir, coconut fiber, or paper. This should be smooth and tightly woven. Rough matting, flooring woven in fat ridges, and any type with loose fibers on the surface can do irreparable damage to a rug or kilim, sometimes even with an underlay, effectively wearing it away with the friction. The rubber soles of shoes can have a similarly detrimental effect.

In a doorway, hallway, or other position where a rug is subject to traffic and wear, one option that will help prevent it being worn is to lay another, smaller rug over it. If you choose or find a rug that is relatively new, the extra wear will actually be beneficial to it, helping to polish the wool. You may well need some sort of anti-slip layer between the two, such as very thin underlay.

It is not only in a position such as a hall or doorway that a rug can be subject to a damaging degree of wear. There are many classic tales of disaster, such as the one that describes the dismay of the owner when he discovers that his favorite rug, which he has laid beneath his desk in his study so that he can enjoy it every day, has been worn away by his feet scuffing as he sits working.

If your rug is old, hold it up to the light before you lay it, to help detect any small holes or areas where the rug has received more wear. Even if it is not yet worn through, examining it in this way may help you prevent further damage. Position the rug on the floor in such a way that the tender spots are protected, or at least not subjected to more wear. Alternatively, take remedial action if the damage is too great to ignore or you are at all worried about it.

There are certain circumstances in which you should think seriously about handing your rug over to a professional to have it mended, such as if the rug is silk, is very valuable, or has been colonized by carpet beetle (you can tell if this has happened because the pile simply falls off the face of the rug, the beetles having eaten the warp and weft threads, if they are woolen, and the back of the knots).

Having a rug professionally mended is expensive, however. There are very few people in the West who are qualified to do the job properly. You are exceptionally lucky if you live near one; more likely, you will have to get the rug to him or her, which can be expensive in itself. There is a danger that the cost of professional mending may be greater than the value of the rug itself.

Do some research before you make a decision: have the rug valued, find a mender (consult an expert or your local reference library), take photographs of the damage, and get some idea of the potential cost of the repair from the person or company who would do it.

In most cases, however, you can do the mending yourself, or at least administer some remedial attention that will prevent the problem becoming worse, and allow you to enjoy the rug for longer without incurring enormous costs. Ordinary clear sticky tape is an amiable friend of the rug owner. Many small frays and holes can be attended to simply by pressing a piece of tape across the back. Lie the rug back down and press any loose threads down into the tape to secure them. This should only be a temporary measure, however.

When an attractive rug of no particular financial value is in very bad condition, with a large hole, you are justified in taking dramatic action. Find or buy a fragment of another, ruined rug. Cut it to size, making the hole in your rug the same size and shape (this means you will have to break the cardinal rule of never cutting the threads of a rug). Insert the piece and sew it in around the edges. Suddenly your old rug has a new lease on life. If you can find a fragment that ties in, in terms of color and pattern, you can congratulate yourself. If not, enjoy the patch for being different.

There are two golden rules to remember when mending a rug yourself. The first is never to cut a trailing thread, however long or loose it seems. The second is never to use glue, of any sort, including any type that claims that it is especially for mending rugs or carpet. Both these actions could cause the rug further damage (and reduce its value, if you ever want to sell it), rather than helping the situation. If a piece ever comes off your rug, for whatever reason, save it and keep it in a labeled envelope if you cannot restore it to the rug.

Choose pure woolen yarn (assuming the rug is wool) in a color that is as close as possible to the area to be mended. A few large, loose stitches may do the job – this is how a hole is prevented from worsening during the washing process in Iran (see the photograph on page 54). Or you may have to rise to some finer needlework, especially if the damage is along the selvage or fringe. Both these parts of the rug are vulnerable to damage, especially the fringe.

Never trim or cut a fringe, even if it looks straggly and unkempt. Simply tuck any long pieces under the rug, and if necessary secure them with a few loose stitches. If a tassel comes off your rug, you may be able to sew it back on in a manner that restores the appearance of the rug, if nothing else. The edge of the rug between tassels can be secured by being oversewn, or use a blanket stitch.

A fringe that has become untidy can also be knotted, though the purists might say you should not do this. Make a series of loose knots, a few threads at a time, across the width of the rug. When you are satisfied, tighten the knots. This is a useful technique for preventing further or worse damage if the weft threads at the end of your rug are threatening to unravel.

A damaged or loose selvage, along the length of the rug, is a worrisome problem. Reattach the warp threads of the selvage, if you can, with regular stitches. In the worst case, it is possible, with dexterity, to create a new selvage. Bind a piece of string with wool yarn of the right color, and sew this on. This is a difficult procedure, and one that takes skill if it is to look at all presentable, but it is worth trying. Without its selvage, a rug has little hope of survival. Not only are the outside warp threads unable to protect the others, but the weft threads too have almost certainly been broken at the edge if the selvage has become detached.

Another problem affecting the edges of a rug is curling. This is usually maddening to the owner, as well as potentially damaging to the rug if it gets uneven wear along the selvage and fringe as a result. Try asking the dealer from whom you bought the rug to have the problem remedied, or try tightening that edge slightly by sewing a taut running stitch along the offending side of the rug.

Alternatively (and this is another solution of which purists might not approve, but it can work), lay a strip of double-sided adhesive carpet tape on the floor under the curl, and press the rug or kilim down. The successful effect may wear off after a while, as the tape's surface gets clogged with dust, so simply replace the tape. A trick to try first is to roll the rug diagonally and leave it thus for a few days to flatten the curl.

If you have chosen your rug yourself and bought it recently, it will probably be in much better condition than one that requires these various types of repair and attention. There are many simple and obvious precautions that will help you to keep it that way.

Furniture, especially heavy pieces, clearly puts pressure on a rug or kilim. This can be reduced if you stand table legs and chair casters, for example, in little glass or plastic cups of the type made for exactly this purpose, sometimes known as "furniture cups" or "caster cups." Metal in particular can not only pressurize but stain a rug, so should be prevented from coming into direct contact.

If you do accidentally make pressure marks on your rug, these should respond to a gentle brush with a damp (not wet) nailbrush. Some people suggest lightly steaming a bad dent and brushing it up every few days. The patch should be allowed to dry thoroughly, as dampness is bad for wool. Wherever possible, it is better to prevent such marks from appearing in the first place.

Move a rug regularly – once a year at least – to prevent its being worn in certain places. It only needs to be moved slightly for this to be effective (unless it is in a position where there is heavy traffic). A runner used on stairs should be moved a small amount at regular intervals without fail, or it will wear on the treads and become useless. If you are enthusiastic, you could keep extra rugs and kilims and change them with the seasons. This is an appealing and successful method of preventing wear on your favorites.

In a temperate climate, there is usually little danger to a rug or kilim from the sun's rays. Extreme conditions, such as lying inside a large, unshaded, south-facing picture window, should be avoided, however (in the northern hemisphere; vice versa in the southern). Even in northern countries, a rug will eventually fade under such circumstances.

It is also easy to forget that, in summer, even in northern countries, the sun shines from early in the morning, often with a burning brightness. A rug exposed to this will eventually fade. A few hours a day over a period of several years can do a surprising amount of harm. The ideal is for the rug to be kept in permanent darkness, but this is clearly not practical or desirable. If a fine rug is kept in a room that is not often used, you could help preserve the vivid colors of the rug by keeping the shutters, blinds, or curtains closed when the room is not in use.

Silk rugs are particularly vulnerable to fading, and they are generally less resistant to wear than wool rugs. As a fiber, silk is strong in relation to its weight, but it becomes delicate with the passage of time. One point in its favor, however, is that it is not attractive to moths.

Though moths can be a problem if the rug is not used and cleaned regularly, the main enemy of rugs and kilims is not moths but dampness. Wool fibers shrink and eventually become brittle if they are not allowed to dry completely. For this reason, it is advisable to keep houseplants away from rugs, and certainly not to place a plant on a rug or kilim. Plants can also introduce mildew to rugs. Cotton is particularly vulnerable to mildew, which is a form of fungus. However, cotton is resistant to rot from damp, and does not shrink like wool under the same circumstances.

LEFT A few bold stitches will temporarily prevent a hole from deteriorating further until it can be properly repaired.

CLEANING AND STORAGE

YOU HAVE YOUR BEAUTIFUL RUG AT HOME, you enjoy it, but in due course it inevitably becomes dirty. The unavoidable question is how to clean it. The answer depends on how dirty it is, and whether there are any particular identifiable stains, but in general you simply clean a rug with a vacuum cleaner.

The old-fashioned, upright sort of vacuum cleaner is not suitable because it has brushes that cause friction and can damage the woolen fibers of a rug over a period of time. A modern cylinder vacuum cleaner is perfectly equal to the job, providing you use a head that is smooth, with no bristles. Move the head across the rug in the direction of the pile, smoothing it down rather than ruffling it up. You can also vacuum the back of a rug, and this is essential if you are hanging a rug on a wall, as moths love to colonize dark, undisturbed places such as the gloom behind a wall hanging.

As ever, the fringe and the selvage are the rug's most vulnerable parts. Be gentle with the selvage, and don't use the vacuum cleaner on the fringe at all. If necessary, brush out the fringe with a soft to medium brush, not a stiff one that could pull out threads or damage their ends. If you do not vacuum your home yourself, it is worth taking trouble to explain about the fringe and selvage to the person who does this job for you.

You can also use a carpet sweeper on rugs (but not one with beating brushes) but, again, not on the fringe and only with care along the edges, being alert to the danger of catching the selvage.

There are two useful and simple ways of cleaning a rug that involve no machinery or technology (or almost none). The first is to pick up your rug and shake it (but not too hard). Do this outdoors in a place where the dust won't offend anyone, or over a hard surface from which the dust and other bits that

drop out can easily be swept or vacuumed. This is a technique that is especially easy to put into action with kilims, since they are lighter than rugs (though a large one is obviously heavier than a small rug).

Alternatively, lay a rug face down and walk on it for a few weeks like this, vacuuming underneath regularly. You may be astonished by how much dust can be removed in this way. With a kilim, which has no pile, vacuum underneath regularly and turn and vacuum occasionally.

Never beat a rug with a stick, and only in one unusual circumstance do the experts say it is acceptable to beat a rug with a carpet beater — the old-fashioned sort that is constructed from bent cane and looks something like a fly swatter. This is in the snow. Providing your snow is crisp and crusty, not wet and sugary, you can lay your rug face down on it and beat, gently but firmly, so that the head of the beater strikes the rug flat. If the tips of the wool pile get slightly wet, don't worry. When you bring the rug indoors, allow it to dry naturally, without being walked on, which would press the dampness down into the structure.

In general, though, beating a rug is a bad idea because it causes it unnecessary, uneven stress. The violence of beating can eventually break the warp and weft threads, causing serious damage and shortening the life of your rug.

If your rug is too dirty to be cleaned by vacuuming, the situation is not irredeemable, although it is obviously worth trying to prevent it from getting this bad. Professional cleaning is expensive and only worth pursuing with a real expert or company specializing in cleaning oriental rugs and kilims. In general, if your rug is in good condition, it is better to clean it yourself by one of the following methods.

144

If your rug is small enough to fit comfortably into the bath, you can simply wash it. Use a baby shampoo, dishwashing liquid, or a gentle soap solution of the type designed for washing wool by hand. Be sure that whatever cleaning agent you use is compatible with the materials from which the rug is made, and that it does not contain bleach or any other whitening ingredient. Don't leave the rug to soak as this will not do it any good. Rinse thoroughly – which may mean ten times or more – until you are satisfied that the water is completely clear and the rug free of soap. Dry gently and thoroughly, away from direct heat.

This method is not suitable for any but a small size of rug. Apart from anything else, a wet rug is extremely heavy, and a larger wet rug is almost impossible for one person to maneuver easily. To wash a rug successfully, you have to be able to lift it into and out of the rinsing water without difficulty, as this is a vital part of the process.

It is also possible to wash and even dry a kilim in the washing machine, however horrified the experts may be. Use the wool cycle and suitable soap, and understand that you are taking a risk.

Alternatively, you can wash your rug as it lies flat on the floor. Place a plastic sheet underneath, and have a generous supply of old cotton towels and a roll of paper towels at hand. Lay old towels flat and smooth on the plastic sheet, and the rug flat on top of this. Make up a solution of clear vinegar with warm (not hot) water and sponge the rug with this so that it becomes damp, not wet.

Dry the dampness immediately by pressing on it with quantities of paper towels. Whenever you clean a rug or kilim, for whatever reason, never rub or scrub, always dab and blot or, if you feel it is necessary, brush gently in the direction of the pile, with a soft to medium brush. As with the bath method, allow the rug to dry thoroughly, without being walked on.

It is well worth looking after your rug so that it does not need an all-over cleaning. Occasional spills are an almost inevitable part of using a rug, however, and there are various ways of dealing with them. The first and guiding rule, if something gets spilled on your rug, is to act quickly.

First, get as much as you can of whatever has been spilled off the rug as quickly as possible. You may need a knife or a spoon to do this or, if the spillage is wet, quantities of absorbent paper towels. In the latter case, use plenty of paper, pressing gently at first, gradually increasing the pressure. Finally, with more absorbent paper towels underfoot, step on the damp patch in order to squeeze out all the fluid that you possibly can from the rug.

If a sugary or greasy matter like butter, cheese, or shoe polish has become ingrained, or a destructive liquid like urine has dried on the rug, you can dilute or soften this by dabbing with turpentine, but do a small test first to ensure that this will not damage the color of the rug (if it has been painted, for example). Alternatively, use a solution of clear vinegar or lemon juice.

Wash the spill, dabbing not rubbing, with a solution of dishwashing liquid in warm, not hot, water, sponging from the edge of the stain inwards so that you don't spread the foreign matter further into the rug. Rinse in the same manner and blot dry. In the case of biological spills like blood, urine, or vomit, or any greasy matter, scrape off what you can before washing with a solution of household ammonia or, if you don't have that handy, a weak solution of bicarbonate of soda.

If chewing gum gets into your rug, do not attempt to remove it until you have chilled it. You can easily do this by filling a watertight plastic bag with ice cubes and covering the chewing gum with this. When it is cold and brittle, scrape off the bits, then proceed as for other spills.

If all this seems alarming, do not worry. Rugs are designed and intended for use. Accidents happen from time to time, and it is better to deal with them when they do than to clog up the fibers of the rug with stain repellent sprays, especially anything containing silicone. Worse still would be to shut your rugs away and not use them at all, for fear of damaging them. Finally, don't be tempted to have your rug or kilim chemically or steam cleaned, as these processes have the extremely damaging effect of removing the natural oils from the wool of which the rug is made.

There are various reasons why you might want to store a rug. If you are lucky enough to have so many rugs that you can change them around with the seasons (or for any other reason that takes your fancy), you will want to keep the ones that you are not using in the best possible conditions. Another reason might be that you have inherited rugs, but have nowhere to use them at the moment. Or you may be packing up the contents of a house prior to moving. There are alternative methods of storage, and the one you choose will depend on your exact circumstances.

The ideal environment for storing rugs is a cool, dry, well-ventilated room with space for the rugs to lie flat. Each rug needs to be thoroughly moth-proofed with crystals (not by being sprayed). Spray of any sort simply applies unwelcome matter to the woolen fibers which gradually works its way into the pile. This not only makes the rug dirty but attracts more dirt, which sticks to it. The crystals should be well crushed and should not touch the pile of the rug, only the back. Lay brown paper under the rug, sprinkle it generously with crystals, lay the rug on top and more brown paper on top of this. And so on, repeating each layer. If the rugs are to be left for more than a few months, they should be checked and the moth-proofing renewed.

Do not fold a rug to store it as this strains the warp over a period of time. Rugs are exported from Iran tied up into bundles, the larger ones folded over, but they remain like this for only a short time. Lying rugs flat requires a generous amount of storage space, even if they are stacked on top of each other. If you don't have the space to spare, but you still need to put a rug away for a while, you can roll it up. Follow the moth-proofing procedure and then simply roll the rug loosely around a smooth, rigid cylinder of some sort, such as a heavy-duty cardboard tube designed to store posters. A friendly fabric shop may let you buy (or have) a discarded stiff cardboard tube that formerly acted as the core of a roll of material. These are usually longer than poster tubes. If nothing else is available, a rod such as a broom handle will suffice, providing it is smooth and clean. Whatever it is made of, the prop needs to be longer than the rug is wide, so that it supports it completely.

Roll the rug, moth-proofing crystals, and paper around the prop, starting at the beginning of the rug, which is to say the end towards which the pile lies, so that the pile does not get flattened during storage.

However you store it, don't forget that your rug is there. If it is a good piece, you have a moment of joy to look forward to, even if it is years before you can take the rug out of storage. When you bring it out into the light, seeing it once again in its full glory, you will experience the pleasure of recognition that comes after the absence of an old friend. A fine rug, well cared for over a span of years, will repay your friendship and care many times over.

RIGHT Nomads' bag facings, each consisting of two matching woven panels, drying in the yard of a warehouse in Tehran. Dealers occasionally have bags such as these on display or for sale.

A NOTE ON BUYING TRIBAL RUGS

Buying rugs is a little like buying antiques – the more information you are armed with when you talk to a dealer, the more comfortable you will feel about your purchase. There are no hard and fast rules, and in many ways your best weapon will be your gut instinct. If you want to buy a genuine tribal rug it is best to shop around, looking at catalogs, comparing prices, and listening to word-of-mouth information. When you see a piece that interests you, ask the dealer questions about its provenance, how it was made, by which tribe, etc. If he is a reputable dealer he will answer your questions gladly – most likely he will be pleased that you have taken an interest in the subject. Be aware of the jargon of buying rugs – knowing the words used to describe the parts that make up a piece or the aspects of pattern will help in two ways, as you can understand the dealer as well as let him know that you are informed (see Chapter Four: Color and Chapter Five: Rug Patterns).

SOME HELPFUL HINTS:

One of the easiest ways to see whether a rug has been made by a genuine nomadic tribe is to look at the back. If it is handmade, the pattern should be as clear on the back as it is on the front. In fact, if the rug is old, the pattern is often clearer on the back as the wool may have faded on the front of the pile. Some machine-made rugs do have a pattern on the back but a close inspection will reveal whether it is machine-made – the pile will have a regular, mechanical pattern.

Tribal weavers do not work from rigid designs, but from their imagination, or from a pattern handed down through generations. Eccentricities and inconsistencies in the pattern of a rug are signs that the piece has been created by a traditional weaver, rather than an anonymous machine.

A rug larger than about 5 × 8 feet is not likely to be a genuine tribal piece, as a nomadic weaver can only work on a loom that can be easily transported. However, some tribespeople have given up the nomadic way of life to work in villages or workshops, so genuine larger rugs do also exist.

When the fringe on an old rug has worn away or been damaged, the kilim (the section of the rug with no pile) or sometimes a strip of the pile border is often unravelled to expose the warps and thus provide yarn for a new fringe. This is easily spotted and can reduce the rug's aesthetic appeal.

RESOURCES

APPRAISERS

American Society of
 Appraisers
(800) 272-8258

The Oriental Rug Retailers
 Association
(540) 832-3353

Posy Benedict
(860) 868-7211

James Ffrench
(212) 717-2502

AUCTION HOUSES

Christie's New York
(212) 546-1187

Sotheby's New York
(212) 606-7996

BOOK DEALERS

Acanthus Books
New York, NY
(800) 827-7614

Myrna Bloom
The East West Room
Dresher, PA
(215) 657-0178

Dennis B. Marquand
 Oriental Rug & Textile
 Books
Culver City, CA
(310) 313-0177

Paul Kreiss
The Rug Book Shop
Baltimore, MD
(410) 367-8194

PUBLICATIONS

Ghereh International Carpet
 & Textile Review
www.ghereh.com
Italy (39) 11 817 8093

Hali Magazine
Hali@centaur.co.uk
London
(44) 171 970 4600

WEB SITES

Oriental Rug Review
www.rugreview.com

Rug News
www.rugnews.com

Turkotek Journal
www.turkotek.com

RUG DEALERS

Asian Trade Oriental Rug
  Center
Tucson, AZ
(520) 326-7828

Persian Mercantile Co.
Berkeley, CA
(510) 843-0552
Toll free (888) 747-RUGS

Mansour
Los Angeles, CA
(310) 652-9999

Sarkisian's
Denver, CO
(303) 733-2623

Tschebull Antique Carpets
Darien, CT
(203) 655-6610

Manoukian Brothers, Inc.
Washington, DC
(202) 332-0700

ABC Carpet & Home
Delray Beach, FL
(561) 279-7777

Marla Mallet Textiles
Atlanta, GA
(404) 872-3356

Minasian Oriental Rugs
Evanston, IL
(847) 864-1010

The Oriental Rug Mart
Peoria, IL
(309) 688-5005

Jacqueline Vance Rugs
New Orleans, LA
(504) 891-3304

D.B. Stock Antique Persian
  Carpets
Wellesley, MA
(781) 237-5859

Mark Keshishian & Sons,
  Inc.
Chevy Chase, MD
(301) 654-4044

Santa Fe Oriental Rugs
Santa Fe, NM
(505) 982-5152

Flying Carpet Fine Rugs &
  Weavings
Taos, NM
(505) 751-4035

Kilim/Linda Miller
New York, NY
(212) 533-1677

The Rug Warehouse
New York, NY
(212) 787-6665

FJ Hakimian, Inc.
New York, NY
(212) 371-6900

Krikor Markarian Oriental
  Rugs
New York, NY
(212) 685-1203

Persian Carpet
Durham, NC
(919) 489-8362

James Opie Oriental Rugs
Portland, OR
(503) 226-0116

Shihadeh
Ardmore, PA
(610) 649-2000

Caravanserai Ltd.
Dallas, TX
(214) 741-2131

Vincent J. Fernandez
  Oriental Rugs
Shelburne, VT
(802) 985-2275

Purcell Oriental Rug Co.
Charlottesville, VA
(804) 971-8822

Michael Wendorf
Alexandria, VA
(703) 739-6648

J.H. Terry Tribal Rugs
Seattle, WA
(206) 233-9766

INDEX

AUTHOR'S ACKNOWLEDGMENTS

The kindness and enthusiasm of many people has helped to make this book what it is, as has the generosity of Nicholas Kneale and Fired Earth in particular, for sending me to Iran, which was the experience of a lifetime as well as providing a unique insight into today's weaving and washing of tribal rugs and kilims in Iran. Writing this book has been an education. I would like to thank all the following: Felicity Bryan and her team, especially Michele Topham; Tessa Clayton; Caroline Exley; Fired Earth; David and Heather Hilliard; Jim and Tracy Hilston; Vivien James and Clare Johnson; Bahman Jamalof, his brother Behruz and everyone at B&B Carpets, Tehran; our Kashgai guides; Nicholas Kneale; everyone at London Oriental Carpets Ltd, especially Nick Oundjian, Wiktor Wyszynski (who read the manuscript enthusiastically for factual accuracy and provided other invaluable information) and Andrew Moxham; Susan and Richard Mosley; Nicky Ingram of the National Trust, Petworth House; Sarah Riddick; William Selka; Hugh, Archie, and Harriet Selka; Jan Walker; Rob Watson; and my companions on the trip to visit and stay with the Kashgai nomads, Jan af Uhr and Peter Wimbush, for their company.

PICTURE ACKNOWLEDGMENTS

All Fired Earth except:
Arcaid/Martin Burgin 134; Arcaid/Petrina Tinsley/Belle 104; Arcaid/Alan Weintraub 130; David Black Oriental Carpets 34, 73, 90, 96, 109; Bridgeman Art Library 15, 20, 21, 23, 24, 27, 29 right, 30, 31, 40, 75 bottom, 76, 77, 108, 137, 139; Hali Publications 14, 16; Robert Harding Picture Library 87, 102, 138; Robert Harding Picture Library/David Brittain 128; Robert Harding Picture Library/Tim Clinch 118; Robert Harding Picture Library/Christopher Drake 111; Robert Harding Picture Library James Merrell 132; Robert Harding Picture Library/John Miller 125; Elizabeth Hilliard 25, 26, 28, 32, 33, 36, 39, 41, 43, 44, 45, 47, 48, 50, 51, 54, 55, 56, 57 bottom, 58, 60, 61, 62, 63, 64, 65 top, 70 bottom, 71, 72, 78, 79, 80, 81 top, 82, 83, 85 top, 93, 94, 95, 101, 131, 143, 146; The Hutchison Library 17, 46, 49; The Interior Archive/Tim Clinch 123; The Interior Archive/Cecilia Innes 114; The Interior Archive/Schulenberg 98, 103, 106, 112, 115, 116, 120, 121, 123, 129; The Interior Archive/Woloszynski 100; The Interior Archive/Herbert Ypma 107, 133; The V&A Picture Library 18, 22; Elizabeth Whiting & Associates 11, 12, 13, 59, 84, 99, 105, 110, 119, 124, 126, 127, 135, 136

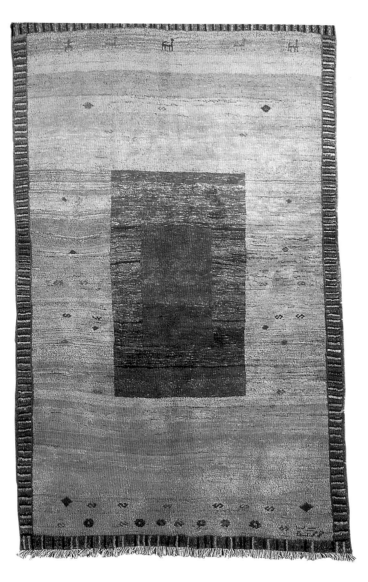

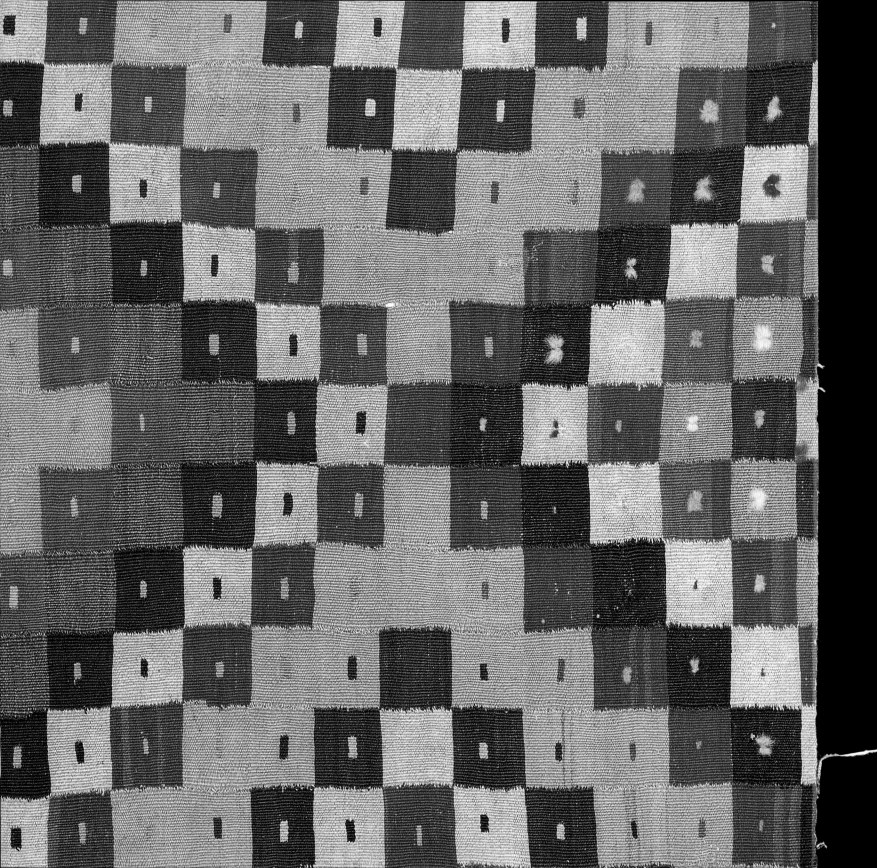